Advance Praise for

Naturally Clean

The Greek root of the word "ecology" means "house." Environmental issues, therefore, are essentially about how we care for our home, or the commons – the publicly owned resources, such as air, water, wildlife and fisheries – that cannot be reduced to private property. Political activism is the best way for concerned citizens to make a difference, but it's also important for each of us to practice an environmental ethic in our everyday lives. *Naturally Clean* is an excellent guide to how we can ensure a safer home for ourselves and our families. I highly recommend this book as an outstanding collection of information for reducing our use of toxic products and protecting our nation's water supply.

— ROBERT F. KENNEDY, JR., President, Waterkeeper Alliance

From the esteemed experts in the field comes the final word on keeping your home clean without jeopardizing your health. *Naturally Clean* by Jefferey Hollender, Geoff Davis, Meika Hollender and Reed Davis covers the history of cleaning products, their effects on humankind, and substitutes for dangerous products in a clear and readable book that would be a worthy addition to anyone's library.

— NELL NEWMAN, President, Newman's Own Organics

Hollender is as important to a healthy home as Trump is to great real estate or Emeril is to spicy food. With his non-alarmist approach, Hollender uses his expertise to deliver an absolute must-read for anyone who cares about creating a healthy household.

— SAMANTHA ETTUS, syndicated columnist and creator of *The Experts' Guide* book series

With *Naturally Clean*, Hollender breaks the mold, showing us all that making money and doing good are not polar opposites. If you want to keep your family and community healthier, your bank balance higher, and your medical bills lower, then read this book!

— DEVRA LEE DAVIS, PH.D.,M.P.H., Director, Center for Environmental Oncology, University of Pittsburgh Cancer Institute, and Graduate School of Public Health; advisory board member, CHEC

If you have children in your home, *Naturally Clean* is a book you should read. It gives invaluable advice about how to keep your home clean while protecting your little ones from hazardous chemicals. It is a very sensible book.

— DR. PHILIP J. LANDRIGAN, Professor and Chairman, Department of Community & Preventive Medicine; Professor of Pediatrics, Mount Sinai School of Medicine; founding board member, CHEC

Redefining what a clean, safe and healthy home really is, *Naturally Clean* is eye-opening and essential to anyone who cares about their own and their family's health.

— MARIA RODALE, Vice Chairman of the Board, Rodale, Inc.

Naturally Clean

The Seventh Generation
Guide to Safe & Healthy,
Non-Toxic Cleaning

Jeffrey Hollender
and Geoff Davis, with
Meika Hollender and Reed Doyle

NEW SOCIETY PUBLISHERS

Cataloging in Publication Data:
A catalog record for this publication is available from the National Library of Canada.

Cover design by Diane McIntosh. Cover images, Photodisc.

Printed in Canada. Second printing July 2006.

Paperback ISBN 13: 978-0-86571-548-6

Paperback ISBN 10: 0-86571-548-3

Inquiries regarding requests to reprint all or part of *Naturally Clean* should be addressed to New Society Publishers at the address below.

To order directly from the publishers, please call toll-free (North America) 1-800-567-6772, or order online at www.newsociety.com

Any other inquiries can be directed by mail to:
New Society Publishers
P.O. Box 189, Gabriola Island, BC V0R 1X0, Canada
1-800-567-6772

New Society Publishers' mission is to publish books that contribute in fundamental ways to building an ecologically sustainable and just society, and to do so with the least possible impact on the environment, in a manner that models this vision. We are committed to doing this not just through education, but through action. We are acting on our commitment to the world's remaining ancient forests by phasing out our paper supply from ancient forests worldwide. This book is one step toward ending global deforestation and climate change. It is printed on acid-free paper that is **100% old growth forest-free** (100% post-consumer recycled), processed chlorine free, and printed with vegetable-based, low-VOC inks. FOR further information, or to browse our full list of books and purchase securely, visit our website at: www.newsociety.com

NEW SOCIETY PUBLISHERS   www.newsociety.com

This book is dedicated with much hope and affection to the next generation, most especially our children: Chiara, Alex, and Meika Hollender, and Genevieve Davis-Chiola. May they know a generous lifetime of play in the fields and forests of a safe and healthy world.

We're donating 100% of our book's royalties to the Children's Health Environmental Coalition's national outreach campaign – Blue Butterfly. CHEC is a national non-profit organization dedicated to educating the public, specifically parents and caregivers, about environmental toxins that affect children's health. Along with the support of celebrity moms Laura Dern and Amy Brenneman, the Blue Butterfly Campaign (www.BlueButterfly.org) will educate millions of Americans across the country about the simple yet critical things they can do to promote a healthier environment and protect children from harm. CHEC's Blue Butterfly Campaign identifies the issues we face and encourages everyone to adopt easy science-based solutions in their homes, day care facilities, community centers, offices, and schools. It's part of CHEC's continuing effort to help parents, teachers, medical professionals, governmental officials, and corporate leaders better understand the responsibility they have to prevent environmentally induced diseases and teach them how to prevent childhood exposure to toxic chemicals in the environment. As proud as I am of our book, I'm even prouder that it's going to support this vital work.

Contents

Acknowledgments

The authors gratefully acknowledge the all too often unsung work of the many dedicated researchers, physicians, activists, and citizens whose commitment to the future of our world, the health of its people and wildlife, and the honest scientific inquiries needed to further both have made this book possible. In particular, we are indebted to the work of Theo Colburn, Dianne Dumanoski, John Peterson Myers, and the staff of Our Stolen Future.org; Dr. Phil Landrigan and the staff of the Mt. Sinai Center for Children's Health and the Environment; Dr. Samuel Epstein and the staff of the Cancer Prevention Coalition; the staff of the Environmental Working Group; Lois Gibbs and the staff of the Center for Health, Environment, and Justice; Annie Berthold Bond; the staff of Environmental Health Sciences; Sandra Steingraber; the staff of Physicians for Social Responsibility; the staff of the Green Guide; the staff of the Children's Health Environmental Coalition; and last but most certainly not least, Martin Wolf for giving us our unofficial degrees in chemical science with unending kindness and infinite patience.

Your works have inspired us. Your knowledge has informed us. And your passionate belief in a better way has been the light by which we've found our own. Without your efforts, our own contribution to a safer world could not have been made. You are each and every one heroes in every way.

An Important Precautionary Preface

This book is based on the Precautionary Principle, an important new environmental philosophy. Though its ideas will be familiar to anyone with a sense of self-preservation, the Precautionary Principle itself was formally created at a 1998 landmark summit conference of scientists, government officials, lawyers, labor activists, and grass-roots environmental leaders at Wingspread in Racine, Wisconsin.

At the heart of this common sense approach to present and future environmental dilemmas lies a simple statement:

> *When an activity raises threats of harm to human health or the environment, precautionary measures should be taken even if some cause and effect relationships are not fully established scientifically.*

Believe it or not, this is a revolutionary idea. That's because when it comes to environmental issues in general and chemical regulations in particular, we here in the United States have based most of our decision-making on a system that says an activity is innocent until proven guilty. In this school of regulatory thought, most activities, whether cutting down a tree or selling a certain chemical, are considered okay to do until someone can prove that they're actually not.

This legal theory has proved to be quite dangerous from a public health perspective. Instead of protecting our families from harm, the current shoot-first-and-ask-questions-later regulatory policies of both federal and local government agencies and lawmakers tend to favor commercial interests. Under this arrangement, products and activities proposed by people and companies are generally allowed to proceed unimpeded, and it's left to the public to definitively prove that they're harmful in some way before they can be stopped. Even when that proof can be established, many times it comes too late. Whether it takes the form of a shattered ecosystem or a prematurely ended human life, the damage has often already been done.

The logic of self-preservation, on the other hand, would seem to dictate that we first prove an activity is safe before we begin it. This latter strategy, after all, is the way we run our lives. We take a certain amount of precautionary care when it comes to our homes and our families, our jobs and ourselves. This is not to say that we don't take personal risks, for indeed we sometimes must in a life well lived, but by and large we carefully pick the chances we choose to take and avoid those that might end in utter ruin.

Such is the thinking behind the Precautionary Principle. The polar opposite of our current regulatory approach, it says that when it comes to environmental issues, we should take a good long look before we leap, and err on the side of caution when making our decisions. When there is doubt about the safety of a product or an action, that product or action should be set aside until those promoting it can prove that it is harmless. That doubt need not have definitive evidence to support it, and if proof that erases this doubt cannot be provided, the product or action cannot proceed.

This is the Precautionary Principle, and it is the foundation of our book. The suggestions and ideas we've placed in these pages are precautionary in nature. In accordance with the Precautionary Principle, it is our fundamental belief that we just don't know enough about many of the chemicals and products that surround us to continue using them. Emerging evidence strongly suggests that these materials may be causing us harm. Until we know what harm is being caused by which chemicals and which chemicals are, by extension, safe, we're going to stop using all of them. We're not going to run through this mine field until we have a map. That's just simple common sense, and you'll find it throughout this book.

When we say, for example, that no conventional chemical cleaning products should be used in your home, we're not saying that every single one of these products will damage your family's health. We're saying that we don't know. Because we suspect that many of them might, we feel it's wise to err on the side of caution and keep all of them out of our lives until solid proof of each specific product's safety can be provided. The stakes are just too high and the questions just too many for us to adopt any other approach.

In the end, it's far easier and a whole lot safer to simply snuff out a match, or never even light it at all, than to extinguish the forest fire it can start. That's why we teach our children not to play with fire. The Precautionary Principle, and this book, simply seek to remind us grown-ups that the lesson still applies.

Introduction
Protecting the Place Called Home

Ordinary household products such as cleansers, cosmetics and paints are now the Los Angeles region's second-leading source of air pollution, after auto tailpipe emissions, air quality officials say.

— *Los Angeles Times*, March 9, 2003

According to a report in the journal Preventive Medicine, by Kenneth R. Spaeth ... data drawn from studies sponsored by the Environmental Protection Agency "indicate that the general population is exposed to unexpectedly high levels of carcinogenic substances in their homes ... The results found that 'the highest personal exposures were 5 to 70 times the highest outdoor levels'" with some toxin levels inside the majority of homes "greater than the levels that qualify as a chemical waste site for Superfund status."

— *New York Times*, January 16, 2001

The Swiss architect Le Corbusier once wrote that "a house is a machine for living in," and indeed, for the typical 21st century home, his statement contains more truth than ever before. Filled with an unfathomable variety of conveniences unknown even a generation ago, the places we call home have become much more than four walls and a roof that together happily conspire to keep our sleeping heads safe from the elements. They have become complex systems with countless interconnected parts and a secret inner life that goes largely unseen by the people who live within.

The many elements that combine to create this inner life represent some of the most remarkable technological advances humanity has ever had the pleasure to experience. In stark contrast to the living conditions endured by even our recent ancestors, we have devices that keep our food perfectly cooled for weeks or frozen for months. On a cold winter's day precious heat is summoned at the touch of a button, and on a hot summer's afternoon we delightfully chill our indoor air instead. At night we need neither candle nor fireplace to banish darkness. In the morning, we awaken at the preset time of our choosing, shower clean in an instantly ready stream of fresh hot water, and emerge into our kitchens to a waiting cup of steaming coffee automatically prepared as we donned our machine-laundered clothes. Throughout the day a vast profusion of extraordinary materials work together to simplify our lives and ensure our optimum comfort. These materials are, in turn, supported by an equally staggering number of high tech potions that might at first glance seem to be the impossible stuff of science fiction and whose real-life wizardry is in actuality no less astonishing.

≈ The fact is, where the majority of consumer chemical products are concerned, we really don't know what the risks are. ≈

Truly, we live in a world of dreams come true. And the machine we call the house plays an increasingly central role in that world. The fulfillment of these dreams, however, has not been without its price, and it's a price that is both steep and often difficult to see.

Our homes derive much of their comfort and the majority of their conveniences from hundreds if not thousands of household products that are made from and filled with exotic new substances and materials. Nowhere is this more apparent than the cleaning cupboard, where we rely on a vast collection of liquids, sprays, waxes, and powders to make our living spaces sparkle. Yet though we use and appreciate these products, their ingredients have largely been invented within our own lifetimes and marketed to the public with minimal short-term and little or no long-term safety testing. It remains to be seen if a lifetime spent among them is safe let alone good for us. These unknowns have turned modern homes into test tubes and the people living inside them into guinea pigs in a vast and uncontrolled research project.

From toilet bowl cleaners to floor polishes, we're living amidst ever increasing amounts and numbers of invisible chemical agents. What are the short- and long-term health consequences of exposure to these materials? What happens inside our bodies when we come into contact with multiple chemicals from multiple sources at the same time? What are the risks for our children? The fact is, where the majority of consumer chemical products are concerned, we really don't know. Because no government agency requires it, the scientific research needed to answer such questions has not been performed. Instead, retailers sell these chemical products on faith, and we ourselves are doing the research as we live, breathe, and raise our families among these materials every day.

Of course, it would be absurd to claim that there have been no health and safety studies of any chemicals whatsoever. Quite the contrary, many materials have, in fact, been studied for many different potential effects. Still, this accumulated research has only assessed the safety of the proverbial tip of the iceberg.

There are an estimated 80,000 different chemical compounds now in use. As of 1995, the National Toxicology Program had tested some 400 of these for carcinogenicity, or 0.5 percent. Based on the results of these studies, researchers were able to estimate that somewhere between five to ten percent of the total number of chemicals in production might reasonably be expected to be carcinogenic. That's 4,000 to 8,000 chemicals that are likely to trigger cancer, to say nothing of the many other diseases and conditions synthetic materials are potentially capable of causing.[1] In the ensuing years, we've made little additional progress determining which of these many thousands of suspect compounds are cause for concern. Indeed, a May 2005 update of the Carcinogenic Potency Database, a global catalog of existing chemical carcinogenicity research at the University of California, listed just 1,485 chemicals as known carcinogens.[2] Clearly, there's much we don't yet know.

What little we *do* know about daily contact with toxic household materials is not reassuring. The evidence that does exist strongly suggests that exposure to many of the common products we take for granted can cause cancer, hormonal disruption, nerve and organ damage, asthma, allergies, and other health problems.

It's a disconcerting conundrum: our homes and many of the products inside them — the "machine" at the very center of our vital efforts to keep our families safe and healthy — may, in fact, be doing just the opposite. The nest we retreat to in our escape from an often dangerous world is likely one of the most hazardous places of all.

This news comes as a genuine surprise to many consumers, and it's easy to understand why. We're conditioned from birth by advertising, product labels, public relations efforts, and other influences to believe that the products we use in our homes are free of serious dangers. We're led to assume that everything we buy has been tested for safety by unbiased scientists adhering to unimpeachable standards, sold by companies that have only our best interests at heart, and carefully monitored by vigilant government agencies dedicated to protecting the public welfare at all costs. Yet upon examination, these and other beliefs don't hold up. Beneath a surface of reassuring presumptions that it seems reasonable to make, there lies an unpleasant truth: many of the materials and technologies we rely on in the modern world are sold to us without any proven record of safety and are exposing us to dangers we can neither see nor imagine. As a result, we are living in a world increasingly awash in toxins and other hazards. And it is making us sick.

This is certainly a discomforting idea, and it's made harder to accept by the fact that there's no one cause to point to, no sole symptom to single out. Instead, there are a million different symptoms, each with its own separate cause. By themselves, these symptoms often don't seem like all that much to be concerned about, and they often don't appear to be related to one another. In the absence of a clearly definable problem with a clearly definable cause, it's only natural for us to think that there really isn't a problem at all.

Unfortunately, there is. It's just not on the front pages of your newspaper. Instead, the evidence that our homes are becoming more hazardous places to live is widely scattered and all too often buried in obscure places like scientific journals that most of us never see. It's hard to find and almost always aggressively discredited by the chemical companies and trade groups whose products' safety is being called into question. In the general absence of widespread media coverage and public alarm, consumers are left to hunt down the clues independently and make their own coherent case that something's wrong. It's a task for which few of us have the time or resources, and even if we could afford the effort, the dots we need to connect are often less than obvious as evidenced by these apparently disconnected facts:

- Forty percent of all Americans will get some form of cancer during their lifetimes,[3] and the American Cancer Society has admitted that the incidence of cancer is expected to double by 2050. Half of all men and almost a third of all women alive today will face this disease.

- Women who work in the home have a 55 percent higher risk of developing cancer and/or chronic respiratory disease than women working outside the home.[4]

- In recent years, over two million household poisonings have been reported annually, 60 percent of which occurred in children under 13 years of age.

- The average sample of breast milk produced by a women in the US contains over 100 contaminants.[5] Some 25 percent of the breast milk supply is now so laden with toxic foreign substances that if bottled and sold as a food product it would violate federal food safety regulations.[6]

- Between 1986 and 1995, the incidence of endocrine and chronic metabolic diseases like diabetes increased 20 percent.[7]

- From 1980 to 1994, the number of people with asthma increased 75 percent and the number of children under four with the disease rose by an explosive 160 percent.[8]

- According to some estimates, a man born between 1970 and 1980 produces three quarters the amount of sperm as a man born between 1950 and 1960.[9]

- Between 1982 and 1995, the number of women of childbearing age who reported difficulty achieving successful conception increased 42 percent. According to the US Department of Health and Human Services, 8 percent of all reproductive-age couples in the country are infertile.[10]

- Allergies are now causing Americans to make 17 million physician visits each year and spend approximately $6 billion a year in allergy-related costs.[11]

- In various surveys, 15 to 30 percent of Americans (44 to 88 million people) report unusual reactions — in the form of headaches, skin rashes, coughs, breathing difficulties, ringing in the ears, and other health problems — to common chemicals such as those found in detergents, perfumes, solvents, pesticides, pharmaceuticals, and foods.[12]

Who would think to put these and other seemingly unrelated anecdotes together to paint a broad picture of an increasingly unhealthy world, let alone conclude that world was waiting for us at home, the very place where we think we're safest from danger? The pieces of this puzzle often just don't seem to go together and the puzzle itself is just too large and too complex for most of us to assemble on our own.

That's why we've written this book. We know where the pieces to the cleaning product puzzle hide. We know how to put them all together. And, most importantly of all, we know how to fix the hidden problems they point to in our homes. We know where the best and safest non-toxic solutions and alternatives lie. And we know how your family can put these solutions to work to build a safer, healthier home. For over fifteen years we've been using this knowledge to help people help themselves and the environment around them. And now we'd like to share it with you.

Our effort to create a better, safer place for all living things started with a simple question: what is a healthy home? We think it's a place built upon a foundation of precaution, one where unnecessary risks are kept to an absolute minimum and living spaces are kept free of hazardous toxins and other dangers. But it's more than that. In our experience, a healthy home must extend into the larger world beyond our windows. By definition it means not only making sure that the activities that take place inside our houses are as non-toxic as possible, but also doing whatever we can to make sure that these activities don't negatively impact the environment outside.

This book is an introductory guide geared toward making it as easy as possible for you to make better, safer decisions and get things done. It's not our intention to provide complex technical examinations of the many issues we'll be addressing within these pages. Though we'll certainly be offering all the latest information you need to understand why particular changes are necessary, why certain chemicals are dangerous, and why some products are better than others, a wealth of available resources already talk about these issues in great detail. (Don't worry, we'll tell you where to find them!) What's missing from the mix is the one thing we intend to provide: an easily used, at-a-glance guide to concrete actions you can take to make your home safer and keep your family healthy.

After a bit of useful background information on the broader issues involved in the art of non-toxic cleaning, we'll dive right into the things you need to care about most. You'll find lists of dos and don'ts, suggestions for healthier options for your home and family, detailed advice on product choices in easy-to-use charts, and resources to help you find the solutions and products we recommend. Take advantage of it all, and you'll have created what we think is the most important thing of all: a healthier place in which to live.

Before we embark on this journey, there's one last thing that needs to be said: our book is not about sacrifices. It's not about making do with things that don't work, settling for arrangements that don't satisfy, or denying your family the comforts and conveniences they want and deserve. It's about finding the alternatives and making the changes that produce the results you're looking for without the unhealthy side effects so often found in today's conventional products. While you may make some small compromises along the way in the name of a safer environment inside and outside your home, they will be mere footnotes in a far larger and more important story. That story is about safe cleaning solutions that work as well as traditional chemical cleaning products, and this book will tell you everything you need to know to make them work for you.

The Case for Change at Home

THE HISTORY OF CHEMISTRY is almost as long as the history of humanity itself. From ancient wines to modern plastics, the science of combining molecules of different substances to produce brand-new compounds has played a crucial role in the human story for countless thousands of years.

In many cases, chemical processes and the substances they create have resulted in immeasurable enhancements to our quality of life. Indeed, were it not for chemistry, our modern world would bear little resemblance to the one we know today. The myriad modern conveniences we enjoy, from our computers to our cars, simply would not exist, and our standard of living would no doubt be far lower.

Clearly, chemistry itself is not a bad thing. It's the kinds of chemicals we make and use that matter. Like most anything else, there is a good side and a bad side to all the molecular manipulation chemists practice. There are safe chemicals, and there are unsafe chemicals. Our problem today is that we don't really know which are which.

Here Come the Chemicals

The modern chemical revolution is a by-product of the petroleum revolution. Experimenting with crude oil, researchers discovered that the chains of hydrocarbon molecules it contained could easily be broken into segments that could then be combined with other materials to create a dizzying array of new substances and materials. When this secret was revealed, the petrochemical age was born, and soon hundreds and then thousands of seemingly miraculous new products were making their way into American homes, each of them hiding any number of never-before-seen substances inside.

At first, no one questioned all this chemistry. In the post-World War II boom of the 1940s and '50s, chemicals and the products made from them were seen as the shining symbol of a modern new prosperity being built by American ingenuity. All across the country, natural was out and synthetic was in. In the kitchen, new time-saving frozen meals and instant just-add-water foods were the height of haute cuisine. In the garden, laborious weeding and bug-infested crops were replaced by a few quick sprays of the latest miracle weedkiller or pesticide. In the closet, wrinkle-free polyester replaced old-fashioned cotton. From plastic wrap to spray wax, people marveled at the amazing wonders science seemed to be inventing every day, and the slogan of the DuPont Company, "Better Living Through Chemistry," was adopted as the unofficial mantra of a grateful nation.

Then, in the early 1960s, the first ripple in the pond of progress appeared. A young marine biologist read a letter in the *Boston Herald* from a reader who claimed that DDT being sprayed to control mosquitoes was killing local songbirds. Curious, the biologist began investigating whether or not there were any ecological side effects being created by the wide-spread use of DDT and other chemicals. The biologist's name was Rachel Carson and her research led to the publication of *Silent Spring,* the book that launched the modern environmental movement.

Until *Silent Spring,* the American public hadn't really considered the effects of chemicals on unintended targets like people and animals. (History would later show that in many instances the chemical industry itself knew things weren't quite right but failed to make this information public.) The outcry following the book's publication was predictable. People were alarmed. Carson was loudly condemned by the pesticide industry. And the scientific community refused to support such "fringe" theories. Fortunately for the rest of us, however, her work was thorough and her conclusions were sound. In time DDT was banned along with several other similar chemicals. Far more importantly, however, Carson succeeded in doing something no one had been able to do before: end America's unquestioning acceptance of the indiscriminate use of chemicals in all facets of modern life.

Our Homes as Test Tubes

Today, there are an estimated 80,000 different chemical compounds being made and used around the world.[1] Each year, the Environmental Protection Agency (EPA) receives approval applications for another 2,000 more. That's more than five new chemicals being created every day.[2] In the United States alone, some 500,000 chemical products are available to consumers,[3] and according to various estimates the average home contains anywhere from three to ten gallons of these toxic substances.[4]

Astonishingly, less than ten percent of these chemicals have been adequately evaluated for human and environmental safety.[5] Of the 2,800 chemicals produced in or imported into the US in amounts over one million tons per year, 43 percent lack even basic toxicity data, and only 7 percent have what was termed by the *San Francisco Chronicle* as "reasonably complete" data regarding their toxicity.[6]

In fact, under the clearly misnamed Toxic Substances Control Act, the EPA is not allowed to require manufacturers to conduct health studies on the new chemicals they introduce unless the agency can demonstrate that a particular substance poses a significant risk. Because such proof can only come from scientific studies that take appreciable amounts of time and money, researchers simply can't keep up with the continual flood of new compounds being introduced, and regulators are forced by a combination of law and circumstance to allow the vast majority into the marketplace with no study and no assurance of safety. The situation has become so extreme that according to the Environmental Working Group, in 2003 less than half of all chemicals submitted for approval to the EPA were backed up by even basic toxicity data, and 80 percent were approved in less than three weeks.[7]

It's for reasons like these that we simply have no idea how our contact with the vast majority of these substances is affecting our health. Yet in spite of this, we continue to use more and more of these compounds in our homes every year. Adding to the problem is the fact that most of the chemicals that enter our homes do so in the form of products that don't tell us what specific substances are lurking inside.

As we said in our introduction, all of these unknowns have the effect of turning our homes into giant test tubes. As we use things like household cleaners, pest control products, plastics, and even products like furniture and electronics, we're conducting an enormous uncontrolled experiment into human chemical exposures, one whose ultimate outcome is largely unknown.

We say "largely" because there is a wealth of emerging evidence that all this chemical use isn't good for us. Scientists are at last beginning to delve into the mysteries surrounding the modern world's myriad of relatively new materials, and they're discovering that many of the things we've surrounded ourselves with are quite capable of causing disease. Taking these findings to their logical conclusion, many in the environmental health community believe our continuous exposure to such substances is responsible for the epidemic rates of cancer, asthma, hormone disruption, and chemical sensitivities the industrialized world is now experiencing.

Household Chemicals and Cancer

Since Congress passed the National Cancer Act in 1971, the incidence of cancer in America has skyrocketed. This family of diseases now strikes 1.3 million people each year and claims 550,000 lives. Forty-four percent of all men and over 39 percent of all women will confront cancer at some point in their lives, levels that are respectively 56 percent and 22 percent higher than they were just a generation ago.[1]

Overall, in the last 30 years, the national incidence of cancer has jumped about 24 percent. If you're thinking that flies in the face of media reports heralding a decrease in cancer rates, you're right. In March of 1998, the National Cancer Institute (NCI) released a report that said five-year cancer survival rates were climbing steadily. This declaration caused the *New York Times* to claim that "the nation may have reached a turning point in the war against cancer." A careful analysis of the statistics used in the NCI report, however, shows that better screening and earlier detection combined with a sharp drop in the number of smoking-related lung cancers was responsible for most of the good news. Strip these factors away, and you're left with more cancer than ever before.[2]

Non-smoking cancer increases noted in the last generation include:

- a 156 percent increase in the rate of malignant melanoma

- a 104 percent increase in liver cancer

- an 87 percent increase in non-Hodgkin's Lymphoma

- a 71 percent increase in thyroid cancer

- a 67 percent increase in testicular cancer

- a 54 percent increase in post-menopausal breast cancer
- a 28 percent increase in brain cancer
- a 16 percent increase in acute myeloid leukemia
- a 26 percent increase in childhood cancers.[3]

Could exposure to chemicals be responsible for all this cancer? Certainly we can't blame every single case of non-smoking-related cancer on environmental pollution, but there is abundant evidence that chemicals are quite likely to blame for an appreciable portion of them. Many believe it's no coincidence that our cancer rates have skyrocketed right along with the introduction and use of synthetic chemical compounds. Interestingly, if you put a chart detailing rising cancer incidences from 1940 onward over a chart illustrating our increasing use of chemicals over the same time period, you'd see a startling parallel. You'd see cancer, a relative rarity in 1900, fast becoming the industrialized world's number one cause of death. At the same time, you'd see some tens of thousands of synthetic chemicals, none of which existed at the turn of the century, coming into production and their use increasing 30-fold. Is this just a coincidence or is it a smoking gun? While that verdict remains to be seen, the facts point in a troubling direction and suggest we shouldn't take any chances:

≈ Interestingly, if you put a chart detailing rising cancer incidences from 1940 onward over a chart illustrating our increasing use of chemicals over the same time period, you'd see a startling parallel. ≈

- One-half of the world's cancers occur among people in industrialized countries, even though those people represent only one-fifth of the global population.[4]

- Breast cancer rates are 30 times higher in the United States than in parts of Africa.[5]

- The International Agency for Research on Cancer has concluded that 80 percent of all cancers are attributable to environmental influences,[6] including exposure to carcinogenic chemicals, many of which are found in household cleaning products.

- In 1995, the National Toxicology Program concluded that based on tests they had conducted, somewhere between five percent to ten percent of all chemicals in production could be expected to be carcinogenic in humans. That's 4,000 to 8,000 different chemicals, almost all of which remain not only unregulated but unidentified.[7]

• Research by Dr. David Sterling conducted in 1991 found that women who work in the home have a 55 percent higher risk of developing some form of cancer and/or chronic respiratory disease compared to women who work outside the home. In presenting his findings to the National Center for Health Statistics, Dr. Sterling noted that "like all occupations, housework has its hazards ... Perhaps the most serious exposure is to modern household cleaners which may contain a number of (both) proven and suspect causes of cancer. The excess prevalence of cancers among homemakers relative to employed women may be due to (these) occupational exposures of homemaking."[8]

• Data obtained from Environmental Protection Agency studies shows that the general population is being exposed to surprisingly extreme levels of carcinogenic substances in their homes. Exposures in some cases were found to be 5 to 70 times higher than the highest outdoor levels. In a majority of homes, the levels of certain toxins were greater than those needed to qualify a location as a Superfund site."[9]

Household Chemicals and Asthma

Cancer is not the only health crisis sweeping America. Asthma has also reached epidemic proportions in the United States. For more than 20 years, the rates of emergency room visits, hospitalization, and death caused by asthma have been rising, especially among children.

According to a 2004 report from Harvard Medical School, between 1980 and 1994 the incidence of asthma among pre-school-aged children rose by 160 percent, more than twice the rate at which it rose in the overall population.[1] Today, the disease is the leading chronic illness of childhood. Some 9 million children have asthma, or nearly 1 in 13,[2] resulting in 14 million missed school days each year[3] and $3.2 billion in treatment expenses.[4] Our kids aren't the only ones facing this challenge. The Centers for Disease Control estimates that 7.5 percent of all adults have asthma, too. That's some 16 million people sick[5] and $9.5 billion in extra health care costs.[6]

What's producing all this asthma? Experts point to all kinds of causes: Car exhaust. Factory emissions. Mold. Dust mites. Cockroach wastes. Tobacco smoke. Even global warming. (Scientists say that as the atmosphere warms, bad-air days increase and more species of molds are able to spread and prosper.) Recently, medical researchers have also begun to explore a possible relationship between asthma and chemical exposures from things like cleaning products.

- An investigation of childhood asthma at Princess Margaret Hospital in Perth, Australia, found that exposure to certain common volatile organic compounds is linked to a higher incidence of asthma. For every ten microgram increase in the concentrations of these cleaning product ingredients per cubic meter of indoor air, the risk of asthma jumped by two to three times.[7]

- A study of 4,521 women conducted at the Municipal Institute of Medical Research in Barcelona, Spain, found a strong correlation between asthma and employment as professional cleaners and attributed 25 percent of the reported cases of the disease to this work. The study concluded that employment in the domestic cleaning industry may induce asthma and that this work has an important public health impact, probably involving not only professional cleaners but also people cleaning at home.[8]

- A Michigan State University study of work-related asthma cases in 4 states discovered that 12 percent were strongly associated with exposure to cleaning products.[9]

- According to *Rachel's Health and Environment Weekly*, experts think that the increase in asthma in industrialized nations may be due to increasing amounts of chemical pollutants present in both outdoor and indoor environments. They believe greater exposures to these pollutants are triggering stronger immune system reactions, which then proceed to manifest as asthmatic reactions to more common substances like dust or perfume.[10]

- A 22-year Finnish study that compared women employed as cleaners to women employed as administrative workers concluded that the cleaning women had an increased risk in developing persistent adult-onset asthma.[11]

- Children with early persistent asthma are ten times more likely to have been exposed to herbicides during their first year of life than children without asthma.[12]

Household Chemicals and Hormone Disruption

In the last few years, scientists have identified a new and quite unexpected way in which the chemicals in household cleaners can affect human health. According to a host of recent studies, many common synthetic substances have the ability to mimic hormones in the body.

Hormones are the body's messengers. Produced in minute quantities by glands like the thyroid, hormones travel to distant points in the body via the bloodstream and deliver chemical messages meant for specific groups of cells. These messages tell the cells what to do and when to do it. Not all cells respond to all hormones. Each type of cell (and the body has thousands) has what are called receptor sites on its surface. These are designed to allow a specific hormone with a specific instruction to attach itself. Once attached, the hormone triggers a reaction in the cell that causes that cell to behave a certain way. Think of it as a lock and key. The cell has locks that only certain keys will fit. The hormones are those keys. If a hormone doesn't fit a cell's receptor site, it goes merrily past and the cell is none the wiser. But if it does fit, it inserts itself and "unlocks" certain functions within the cell. In this way, hormones act as the body's control system. They regulate its operations and growth, and are a primary reason why complex multicellular life forms like human beings are able to exist.

It's important to note that hormones are extremely powerful substances often measured in parts per trillion in the bloodstream. They're so powerful, in fact, that one of their functions upon arrival at a target cell is to have the cell send a chemical message back to the originating gland to stop producing the hormone itself. Like a thermostat shutting down a furnace when the house has been warmed, hormones, by necessity, turn themselves off because too much of any given one in the bloodstream could cause harmful effects. It's a mechanism that underscores both the incredible beauty of the human body and the exceedingly delicate balancing act that maintains its health.

Researchers have discovered that many of the chemicals in household cleaners and other consumer products have molecular shapes very similar to the shape of certain hormones. This similarity allows these chemical "keys" to fit into many cells' hormonal "locks." Once in place, these synthetic imposters can either prevent legitimate hormones from attaching or they can inadvertently deliver the wrong message to the cell, which can't tell them apart from a real hormone. The result can be cellular confusion. Cells divide when they shouldn't or fail to grow when they should. Functions they are supposed to assume go unperformed or occur at the wrong times.

Hormone disruption, or endocrine disruption as it's also known, is not itself a disease. Rather, it is an underlying cause of other conditions like cancer, reproductive problems, and developmental disorders. This means we're not ever likely to see studies declaring, for example, that the incidence of hormone disruption is rising or falling. Rather, we need to recognize that it is a condition lurking behind other health problems and that we're going to have to read between the lines to find clues to the mayhem it may be creating. Increasing numbers of scientists believe those clues are now emerging in the form of recent headlines about the alarmingly early onset of puberty now occurring in young girls, declining sperm counts in men, and other strange reproductive and developmental trends.

Hormone disruption is also an extremely new area of medical study, one that's only surfaced in the last few years. With the exception of a very few recent studies, the scientific community hasn't yet identified what precise effects chemical mimicry of hormones is causing in human beings. Instead, most of the available research to date has focused on which chemical compounds demonstrate an ability to pose as hormones and the effects that these substances have on animals.

- The number of fish with both male and female characteristics is on the rise. Researchers cite sewage effluent released into rivers as the culprit. The effluent contains alkyl phenol ethoxylate, a potent estrogen-like chemical commonly found in household detergents. Scientists have linked this chemical to the birth of fish that are half-male, half-female.[1]

- That same surfactant, alkyl phenol ethoxylate, has been found to break down in the body into p-nonylphenol, an endocrine disruptor.[2]

- Phthalates, a ubiquitous group of compounds used in PVC and other plastics, perfumes, hairsprays, lubricants, wood finishes, medical supplies, footwear, flooring, inks, product packaging, food wrap, and children's products, have been found to interfere with the hormones estrogen and androgen.[3]

- Malathion, a common insecticide used in public insect control programs, consumer pest-control products, and head lice treatments has been found to interfere with thyroid functioning.[4]

- According to a study conducted by the University of Missouri-Columbia and North Carolina State, Bisphenol-A (BPA), a common chemical in polycarbonate plastics like those used to make things like baby bottles, aluminum can linings, and food storage containers causes premature puberty in mice. Unborn mice exposed to low levels of BPA reached puberty earlier and weighed 20 percent more than normal, leading researchers to conclude that prenatal BPA exposure is a potential factor in the alarming increase in premature puberty and obesity problems now being seen in young girls.[5]

≈ Researchers have discovered that many of the chemicals in household cleaners have molecular shapes very similar to the shape of certain hormones. ≈

- In a study conducted at Kings College in London, researchers studied the impact that three common estrogen-mimicking pollutants and one natural estrogen had on mouse sperm. Though the synthetic estrogen-like compounds were found to be 1,000 times weaker than the natural estrogen studied, they were 100 times more potent when it came to their effect on the sperm, which were so overstimulated by their contact with these pollutants that they were often exhausted early in their life cycle and unable to complete their mission.[6]

Household Chemicals and Multiple Chemical Sensitivities

In the 1980s, a new condition called multiple chemical sensitivities (MCS) began to appear in people in the industrialized world. Also known as *chemical sensitivities* or *environmental illness,* its symptoms were wildly varied, often extreme, hard to concretely identify, and even harder to ascribe to any particular cause.

In fact MCS was so unlike anything that had come before it that many doctors and researchers initially refused to believe it existed at all. Like Gulf War Syndrome, it seemed so outlandishly bizarre and so variable from case to case that most medical professionals believed that MCS sufferers were simply misdiagnosed or suffering from some extreme form of hypochondria.

As more and more victims stepped forward, however, the condition could no longer be dismissed by the traditional medical community. Today, though it remains little understood, MCS is increasingly acknowledged as a legitimate condition. Most consider it an ailment or family of ailments whose typical symptoms include prolonged fatigue, memory difficulties, dizziness, lightheadedness, difficulty concentrating, depression, lethargy or grogginess, loss of motivation, feeling tense or nervous, shortness of breath, irritability, muscle aches, joint pain, headaches, head fullness or pressure, chest pains, difficulty focusing the eyes, and nausea.

Although research is ongoing into this emerging disease, MCS seems to have two stages. In the *onset stage,* the disease is initiated by either a single high exposure to a certain chemical (for example a chemical fire, spill, or accident) or by repeated low-level exposure to the chemicals in everything from cleaners to carpets. After these initiating exposures, the *chronic phase* begins and ongoing symptoms are then triggered by extremely low exposures to any number of chemicals that may or may not include the chemical that originally caused the condition. An adverse reaction to one chemical creates such a severe response to so many others that the victim can only be treated via isolation from as many synthetic materials and compounds as possible.

Obviously, not everyone who is exposed to chemicals gets MCS. Researchers still have no real idea why some people acquire it while others exposed to the very same conditions do not. Recent evidence suggests the nervous system (or perhaps the nervous and immune systems together) somehow becomes sensitized by the initiating chemical exposure or series of exposures. In this way, MCS can be seen as a severe-onset allergy with multiple triggers that produce extensive and highly variable reactions often far out of proportion to the size of the exposures themselves.[1]

In various surveys, 15 percent to 30 percent of Americans (some 44 to 88 million people) report they are unusually sensitive or allergic to certain common chemicals in this way. These sensitivities are triggered by detergents, perfumes, solvents, pesticides, pharmaceuticals, and even dry-cleaned clothes. An estimated 5 percent (14.7 million people) have been diagnosed by physicians as being especially sensitive.[2] Many of these people react so strongly that they can become physically disabled from very low exposures to common substances.

Researchers Nicholas Ashford and Claudia Miller have suggested MCS is not the best name for this condition because it fails to reflect the importance of the initiating chemical exposure. They suggest that Toxicant-Induced Loss of Tolerance (TILT) better describes the true nature of the illness since an initial exposure to a single chemical leads to the loss of tolerance to a far wider variety. Just as different infectious diseases can all cause a fever, so can different initiating chemical contacts all cause a sensitivity to chemicals in general.

The Burden Our Bodies Bear

There's one final piece of evidence that clearly indicates the need for changes in the way we live. That piece of evidence is something called the *body burden*.

As ever increasing amounts and types of different industrial chemicals are being manufactured and used, the environment is becoming increasingly contaminated by the pollution these chemicals create. This is because many of the synthetic chemicals made today do not easily break down into harmless bits and pieces as natural materials do. Instead, they resist decomposition, and once they're introduced into our air, water, and soil, they tend to remain there for long periods of time. This persistence means that as more of these chemicals enter our environment, they accumulate in ever larger amounts. In short, we're unintentionally adding chemicals to our environment faster than it can break them down and remove them, and so the total amount of chemicals the environment contains is rapidly growing. In practical terms, these increasing levels of environmental pollution mean that people are encountering higher and higher amounts of unseen chemical pollution much more often in the course of daily life.

A large number of these compounds are also fat-soluble, that is, they are easily absorbed by fats and oils. The fats into which these chemicals readily dissolve include human fatty tissues. But fatty tissues aren't the only place in the human body in which persistent chemicals tend to collect. They are also stored in muscles, bones, and brain and organ tissues. Once absorbed by our bodily tissues, these toxic compounds tend to remain there because they aren't easily broken down and excreted.

Whenever a new persistent chemical molecule finds its way inside us, it's added to those already stored there. The result is our body burden, the sum total amount of accumulated toxic contaminants we have ingested over time by breathing polluted air, eating food with toxic residues, drinking contaminated water, and exposing our skin to dangerous chemicals.

In the last few years, scientists have begun to examine our body burdens in detail, and what they've discovered is discomforting at best. They've found that the body of the average American is littered with countless toxic chemicals.

- According to an EPA study of human fatty tissue samples, every American man, woman, and child carries at least 700 pollutants in his or her body.[1]

≈ According to an EPA study of human fatty tissue samples, every American man, woman, and child carries at least 700 pollutants in his or her body. ≈

- A 2002 study conducted by the Centers for Disease Control checked blood and urine samples from over 2,500 statistically representative Americans for 116 different chemicals including pesticides, phthalates, PCBs, dioxins, and heavy metals. Researchers found a wide variety of different kinds of contamination, including some from materials that have been banned for decades. Five percent of the 1,007 women in the study, for example, had 49.4 parts-per-billion or more of cancer-causing PCBs in their samples. Measurable amounts of DDT breakdown products were found in virtually everyone, including people born after this pesticide was banned. And levels of certain developmentally damaging phthalates, a toxic component of everything from toys to personal care products, were found in children at twice the level found in adults.[2]

- A 2003 study conducted by the Mount Sinai School of Medicine in New York, the Environmental Working Group, and Commonweal found a total of 167 different chemicals, pesticides, and pollutants in the blood and urine of 9 volunteer test subjects. None of the volunteers worked with chemicals on the job or lived near an industrial facility, yet each one had an average body burden of 91 contaminants, many of which came from insecticides, personal care products, and household cleaners. Of the 167 chemicals found, 76 cause cancer in humans or animals, 94 are known to be toxic to the brain and nervous system, 77 are capable of harming the immune system, and 79 cause birth defects or abnormal development, to name just a few of the bodily functions affected by the chemicals that were identified.[3]

8

Toward Safer Homes and Healthier Families

In the conservative realm of science, nothing can be certain without proof, and the only acceptable kind of proof is the certainty of a clearly identifiable effect created by a clearly identifiable cause. Though understandably strict, this rigid parameter makes it quite difficult to develop an irrefutable case that our modern chemically-intensive lifestyle harms human health. The task of linking any of over 80,000 chemicals to any of thousands of human diseases and/or damage to a similar number of hormonal and other bodily functions falls just this side of impossible.

Producing such a link is made even more difficult by the fact that we are rarely if ever exposed to just one chemical compound. Instead we encounter dozens in the course of daily life and more often than not are exposed to more than one substance at a time. To try to connect the countless combinations of chemicals to which we're exposed to specific health conditions is a goal that's utterly unachievable. (For more information on this impossibility see our section on synthesis in Chapter 11.)

As a result, only in a relatively few cases can we say for certain that chemical x causes condition y. In the absence of such undeniable proof, the chemical industry is quick to reassure consumers that absolutely no evidence exists that the products they're buying and using are hazardous to human health. Little if any regulatory action needs to be taken, they say, because it's simply not been proven that anything unhealthy is happening. Even scientists must often reluctantly but honestly admit that they lack any concrete evidence that this or that substance is harmful in any specific way.

On the face of it, these statements are true. But the simple fact that no evidence of harm exists for a particular chemical does not in any way translate into proof of its safety.

This leads us to a very important question: how much evidence is actually necessary in order to make the case that we should be far less tolerant of the use of chemicals in our homes? Might we not have enough already?

After all, there are some things we do know. We know that our use of chemicals has skyrocketed in the last 50 years. We know that today we're making and using greater amounts and more different kinds of these synthetic compounds than at any other time in human history. We know that our bodies have been and continue to be contaminated by hundreds of these chemicals. We know that many of these pollutants can cause cancer, hormonal disruption, reproductive and developmental disorders, neurological problems, organ damage, and other health problems.

We also know that during the very same period of time that our use of chemicals has exploded, cancer has reached epidemic proportions, and asthma has crippled vast numbers of our children. We know that unusual hyperallergic reactions have inexplicably developed among significant portions of the population. We know that as a species we've been slowly getting sicker.

Isn't it logical to believe there might be a connection between these things? Though we may lack overwhelming scientific proof, isn't it reasonable to think that our rising use of chemicals and our rising rates of illness are somehow related? Given that the stakes are as high as they can possibly get, isn't it prudent to suggest that it might be wise to stop using these chemicals and the products that contain them until we're sure they're safe for our families?

More and more people think that it would be. From environmental experts to medical doctors to average homeowners, millions of people throughout the industrialized world believe that the case for change has now been made. Though many pieces of the chemical puzzle remain unplaced, they agree that we've got enough evidence on the table to get a very good idea of the picture that's taking shape. That picture says that there is some very serious risk involved in the indiscriminate use of household chemicals. And that this risk isn't worth it.

If we've got someone we love or something we can't afford to lose, we don't take unnecessary chances. If our child is in the back seat, we don't drive like a maniac. If we've got only one copy of the novel we spent years writing, we don't take it on a whitewater rafting expedition. We don't let our dogs off the leash in traffic or play catch with family heirlooms. Better safe than sorry, you know. It's just simple common sense.

This same common sense must now be applied to the chemicals, technologies, materials, and products we use in our homes. Connect all the dots, and it's clear we've got more than enough proof that the time for a healthy change has come.

Household Chemistry 101

IF YOU'RE ANYTHING LIKE US, you probably remember high school chemistry class with something less than whole-hearted enthusiasm. For many, the endless hours spent among our school's test tubes and beakers are recalled as a confused jumble of incomprehensible formulas, confounding concepts, experiments that produced either noxious odors, singed hair, or both, and headache-inducing periodic tables that might as well have been written in ancient Egyptian.

If that's true for you, we have good news: this section of our book is going to be nothing like that! That's because the chemistry that surrounds us in our homes is fairly easy to understand. It requires nothing more than a simple lesson in how the substances and materials we use in our homes behave once they get there and what they do after we're done with them.

What happens, for example, when you use a petrochemical spray cleaner around your bathroom and rinse its remains down the sink? What happens in your home's atmosphere when you install a rug and fill your home with that "new carpet" smell? The answers to these and many other everyday questions aren't nearly as complicated as you might think. And that's a very fortunate thing because knowing a few simple things about the science that lies behind household products can go a long way toward keeping you safe from the health hazards many contain.

9

A Short History of Chemicals

Hundreds of millions of years ago, Earth was covered by vast oceans filled with billions upon billions of tons of tiny prehistoric plants and animals. As these plants and animals died, their remains settled to the bottom of these ancient seas where they were quickly covered by decay-preventing sediment. Over the eons, thousands of feet of sediment and rock accumulated above them, and the resulting heat and pressure of this geological burial turned these layers of dead plants and animals into a viscous black material we call petroleum.

On a chemical level, the earth's petroleum consists of many long strings, or chains as they're called, of carbon atoms bonded in various configurations with hydrogen atoms. These combination hydrogen and carbon molecules are called *hydrocarbons*. In their raw state, petroleum's long chains of hydrocarbons don't have much use. But when they're broken into shorter chains, we get useful products like propane, butane, gasoline, heating oil, lubricants, and ethylene, the building block of everything from plastics to detergents. This process of breaking long chains of petroleum into shorter chains, or individual products, is called cracking, and it's accomplished by applying a combination of heat, pressure, and catalytic materials to raw petroleum.

Once petroleum has been cracked, all the products it contains are jumbled together in a thick soup. They have to be separated, and this is done by boiling the mixture of chains, a process called distillation. Fortunately for the modern world, each individual product, whether it's gasoline or propane, boils at a different temperature. When the thick soup is slowly heated, the different products within it boil off one after another as their respective boiling points are reached. (This is what's happening inside those strange looking towers we see at refineries). Once released from the soup, each product is captured and condensed back to a liquid state. This distillation produces surprisingly pure products, which are cleverly called "petroleum distillates."

Many petroleum distillates can be used without further processing. Liquid petroleum gas (LPG), gasoline, diesel fuel, and heating oil are petroleum distillates that are used to produce energy. Other products, called naphthas, are used as solvents on greases and tars that will not dissolve in water. Still other petroleum distillates, like ethylene, are combined with a wide variety of other substances to create everything from plastics to pesticides. Together, these distillates are the backbone of the chemical revolution that took place in the last century.

At about the same time that scientists were discovering all the things that could be made out of petroleum hydrocarbons, they were also finding out that a similarly impressive number of materials could be made out of chlorine, a basic element discovered in 1774 by Swedish scientist Carl Wilhelm Scheele.

As it happens, chlorine is an equally ideal raw material with which to work. Once used solely for sanitizing and bleaching, chlorine was discovered by chemical engineers of the early 20th century to be an element that easily combined with a wide variety of other substances to create new materials called *chlorinated compounds,* which held great potential as building blocks of often astounding new products.

Chlorinated compounds exhibit a number of useful characteristics. Chief among these is durability. Scientists discovered that the strength of the molecular bonds created between the chlorine atoms and the carbon atoms that make up many chlorinated compounds were often quite strong. Chlorinated chemicals are very tough molecules. They tend to resist decay, stand up to adverse conditions, and last for an extremely long time. This remarkable stability makes them incredibly versatile, and chemical engineers have exploited this characteristic to produce all kinds of long-lasting products and materials.

Today, there are about 15,000 chlorinated compounds in commercial use. Many of them are made by combining chlorine with hydrocarbons from petroleum to create materials collectively known as *chlorinated hydrocarbons.* Even a cursory look around the typical home will reveal hundreds of different chlorinated hydrocarbons being used in everything from vinyl siding to household cleaners.

10

Top of the POPs

In addition to their remarkable stability and longevity, scientists have recently discovered another characteristic common to chlorinated hydrocarbons. They are often associated with chronic health problems. More so than most other families of chemicals, chlorinated hydrocarbons are associated with cancer, hormonal disruption, developmental and reproductive disorders, and a number of other serious conditions. In fact, so many chlorinated hydrocarbons seem so remarkably capable of causing so many human illnesses that environmental scientists in the late 1990s decided to create a brand-new category of chemical pollutant in which to place them.

That category is called POP, an acronym for Persistent Organic Pollutant. This label has been officially adopted by the United Nations Environmental Programme, but not by the United States Environmental Protection Agency. Instead, that agency uses the acronym PBT, which stands for Persistent, Bioaccumulative, and Toxic, to describe similar substances. The classifications POP and PBT are very similar if not interchangeable, and the same chemicals appear on lists of both. Because the international community has chosen POP as its preferred label (and because it's easier to say), we're choosing it as well.

The creation of the POP classification for chemicals is notable because it's the first time that environmental scientists have chosen to group chemicals together not on the basis of their molecular similarities but their behavioral similarities.

POPs include many pesticides, household and industrial chemicals, and by-products of a variety of manufacturing and waste incineration processes. To earn the POP designation, a chemical must:

- persist in the environment

- build up in body fat and accumulate in ever higher levels as it migrates up the food chain (this is called bioaccumulation, and we'll have more on it in a minute).

- travel efficiently in the atmosphere and global waters

- be linked to serious hormonal, reproductive, neurological, and immune disorders.

Because of their unique ability to spread in the environment and cause disease in animals and humans, POPs are now getting closer looks from regulators and others involved in keeping people safe from harm. In spite of this increased scrutiny, however, they continue to be made, used, and found in a number of common household products like cleaners and pesticides.

11

Bad Behavior

Although POPs are especially toxic, they aren't the only kind of household chemical that can cause harm to human health. Many other commonly used substances are also quite capable of exhibiting bad behavior. Understanding this behavior is largely a matter of understanding just five fundamental ideas. Learn these basics and you've gone a long way toward learning most of what you need to know about the basic problems with many household chemicals.

Biodegradability

Everyone is familiar to some extent with the concept of biodegradability. It's the force behind our compost piles and the reason why autumn's leaves are largely gone come spring. When we talk about the biodegradability of a material or substance, we're talking about its ability to be broken down into its smallest component parts. This decomposition can be caused by hungry microorganisms, whose digestive systems break compounds apart into simpler substances. It can also be caused by light via a process called photolysis. Or a material can be broken down by contact with water in a process called hydrolysis.

Biodegradability lies at the heart of nature's sustainable recycling system. Once created, everything from trees to deer doo-doo is eventually broken down by various natural forces into its most basic parts, which then become the building blocks for new life that itself will some day similarly decay.

When it comes to household chemicals, biodegradability is generally a good thing. The faster a given hazardous substance decomposes into safer bits and pieces, the less time it has to hang around and cause harm to human health. But when that biodegradation is slow or nonexistent, the material in question remains intact to wreak continued havoc long after we've finished using it.

This is why manufacturers often tout their products' "biodegradability" on product labels. But there are three things to keep in mind when considering this claim. One is that even though a material or substance may seem to disappear, that doesn't always mean it's been safely biodegraded. Remember the so-called "biodegradable" trash bags that were sold in the late 1980s? The manufacturer claimed that sunlight biodegraded these bags. But when studied, researchers found that the bags, which contained a cornstarch additive allegedly appealing to microorganisms, were simply breaking up into pieces of plastic too small to be seen with the naked eye. The plastic hadn't really decomposed. Each bag just broke apart into a zillion bits of microscopic size.

The second thing to remember is that the usefulness of biodegradability is wholly dependent on time. If a substance takes 1,000 years to fully decompose, it's technically 100 percent biodegradable, but much less so in reality. For example, a chemical that takes just 5 days to decay is far less worrisome and far more biodegradable than a chemical that takes 5, 50 or 500 years to break down. Just because something is biodegradable doesn't guarantee it's safe! Even the most hazardous and long-lived chemicals will eventually biodegrade, but because the process may take many lifetimes, we can't count on this kind of biodegradability to protect us once those chemicals are made and used.

The third point to keep in mind is that a substance may be quite biodegradable but only under certain conditions, like those found in a carefully controlled compost pile or supervised municipal waste facility. When these specific conditions do not exist, the material in question will biodegrade very slowly or not at all. These kinds of biodegradable materials should also be considered essentially non-biodegradable because from the standpoint of common consumer use the conditions they need to decompose are not easily found.

Instead, truly biodegradable products will be labeled "readily biodegradable." This designation means that the material in question will easily and completely break down in a wide variety of different conditions, including those likely to occur when consumers dispose of the product in common ways.

Persistence

Persistence is the other side of the biodegradable coin. If a substance or material does not readily biodegrade, it's said to be persistent. Unfortunately, common household products are frequently made from persistent chemicals. Many of the toxic ingredients they contain and the hazardous materials they're made from strongly resist nature's attempts to break them down. From the chunk of Styrofoam your new computer was packed in to the chlorinated hydrocarbon hiding in your oven cleaner, once we make and use these persistent compounds, they're with us for the duration. Some toxins, like many of the POPs we talked about earlier, can take hundreds of years to decompose. And along the way, they're more than capable of spending a lifetime in our bodies, a fact that leads us to the term bioaccumulation.

Bioaccumulation

Bioaccumulation occurs when animals and human beings ingest a chemical over time (usually in very small doses) via air, food, and/or water, or absorption through their skin. If the ingested chemical is persistent, it tends to build up, or bioaccumulate, in bodily tissues.

Say, for example, that the milk you drink contains dioxins and that you ingest a single dioxin molecule every day for a week with your morning cereal. Because dioxins are persistent, they won't be broken down and excreted by your body. Instead, these fat-soluble molecules will be attracted to and absorbed by your body fat. This means that at the end of our hypothetical week, you will have bioaccumulated seven dioxin molecules in your body. The following week you ingest seven more dioxin molecules with your daily breakfast. These 7 are added to the previous week's total to create a grand total of 14 dioxin molecules now stored in your body's tissues. As your body absorbs and retains chemical pollutants over time in this way, it adds each new amount to that which is already there and you establish the body burden we discussed in Chapter 7: the ongoing total amount of bioaccumulated materials within your bodily tissues.

≈ Because POPs tend to be both bioaccumulative and highly toxic, their presence in our bodies is one of the most important environmental health issues of our time. ≈

Bioaccumulation also refers to a material's slowly increasing presence in animals and people as it moves up the food chain. This process is also called *biomagnification.* Here's an example that illustrates the idea: A group of ten planktons ingests five dioxin molecules each. These plankton are then eaten by a tadpole who itself has ingested five dioxin molecules. As a result of all this eating, our tadpole now has 55 dioxin molecules in its body. When the tadpole is eaten by a fish, the fish's body adds the 55 dioxin molecules accumulated by the tadpole to its own toxic storehouse. And if the fish is eaten by a human being, that person gets more than a meal. He or she also ends up eating all the dioxins eaten by the plankton, the tadpole, and the fish combined. The dioxins have bioaccumulated in ever-increasing amounts as they moved up the food chain.

Many of the chemicals we encounter in the course of daily life can easily bioaccumulate inside our bodies. Of particular concern are those in the POP family. Because POPs tend to be both bioaccumulative and highly toxic, their presence in our bodies is one of the most important environmental health issues of our time.

Synthesis

Synthesis occurs when the chemicals in the different products we use around the house come into inadvertent contact with each other and accidentally combine to create brand-new compounds. These new substances can sometimes be more toxic than any of the original chemicals. For example, many people are surprised to learn that combining ordinary household chlorine bleach with ammonia will cause these two chemicals to immediately react with each other and produce a deadly gas. Reactions like these between any number of the compounds found in the many products we use have great potential to create new hazards. And in most cases we can't see the uncontrolled chemical reactions that take place during accidental synthesis; nor are there any clues that something new and potentially toxic has been created. In fact, we simply have no idea what kind of compounds are being unknowingly created when chemical products meet each other in the laboratory called home, and there could be millions. According to Peter Montague, editor of *Rachel's Health and Environment Weekly,* in any given group of 1,000 different chemicals there are 41 billion possible combinations of groups of 4. Even if we could achieve the utterly impossible and test a million of these combinations for safety every year, it would still take scientists 41,000 years to finish the job.[2] Synthesis also occurs when the chemicals found in cleaning products interact with materials found in the environment. Chlorine, for example, can combine with natural organic materials found in dirt and soils to create a variety of carcinogenic chlorinated hydrocarbons, including toxins like chloroform and trihalomethanes.

The terpenes found in pine cleaners and other products like air fresheners are another case in point. These compounds help give those products their scents, but they easily react with the low levels of ozone (created by reactions between fossil fuel exhaust and sunlight) typically found inside and outside urban homes. These unseen reactions create formaldehyde, carbonyls, and other toxins, and they continue for hours after the product containing the original terpenes has actually been used.[3]

Potentiation

Synthesis isn't the only thing that can happen when chemicals accidentally meet on surfaces and in the air inside our homes. Interactions between the chemicals found in different products can sometimes enhance the potential for harm of any or all of the individual chemicals involved. This process is known as *potentiation*. For example, the solvent acetone, which is found in products like nail polish removers and waxes, has been shown to increase the liver damage caused by carbon tetrachloride (a household chemical now thankfully banned), even though acetone itself doesn't harm the liver.[4]

In an experiment studying the effects of combinations of endocrine-disrupting chemicals, Andreas Kortenkamp, a researcher at the University of London's School of Pharmacy, created a mixture of eight known synthetic hormone mimickers typically found in water supplies and consumer products and applied this blend to yeast cells altered to have human estrogen receptors on their surface. Each of the individual hormone-mimicking substances was present in this mixture at half the concentration level previously identified as triggering observable hormonal effects. Because none of the chemicals were present in the amounts needed for them to create hormone-like effects, the mixture should theoretically have had no impact on the yeast cells. Instead, Kortenkamp found that "a strong effect" was created by the combination of chemicals as measured by the production of an enzyme produced whenever the yeast cells' estrogen receptors were triggered.[5]

Acute vs. Chronic
How We're Exposed to Household Chemicals

The chemicals in household products from cleaners and pesticides to toiletry items and home furnishings can be absorbed through the skin, inhaled into the lungs, or ingested via the stomach. This contact occurs both during and after the actual use of the product. Though our exposure to the hazardous substances contained in these products is obviously greatest when the product is being used, it doesn't end there. Many products leave residues behind. Others evaporate some or all of their ingredients into the air we're breathing. Some suspend themselves in that same air and later come to rest on food, clothing, and other surfaces. In these ways, our exposure to the chemical dangers a product holds often continues well past the time of its actual use. These exposures fall into one or both of two broad categories: acute exposures and chronic exposures.

An *acute exposure* is a single, massive overexposure to a product or chemical. This is the kind of danger that cleaning product labels tend to warn us about. (See Chapter 16 for more about product labels.) Poisonings are the most common and well-known acute effect. Indeed, in 2003, 90 percent of all reported poisonings in America occurred at home and the second leading reported cause of these poisonings (after analgesics) was household cleaners.[1] But poisonings are only one kind of acute event. Acute exposures can also result from chemical contact with skin, eyes, or mucous membranes. Or they can occur through inhalation of large amounts of chemical fumes.

Chronic effects are much different. They result from repeated low-level exposures to a chemical or product over an extended period of time. For example, you may inhale just a teeny tiny bit of household spray wax during your weekly cleaning. Many years of such regular ingestion create a chronic exposure from which a negative health effect often arises.

Chronic health effects are much more difficult to verify than acute effects, which tend to be immediate, severe, and clearly linked to a specific chemical contact. This is because it usually take years if not decades for chronic effects to manifest themselves. By the time a chronic exposure has finally built to the point where a health problem is noticed by the victim, so much time has passed and so many other variables and potential causes have been encountered that pinpointing the exact source of the problem may be impossible. More importantly, it is often too late to do anything meaningful to reverse the condition itself and aid the sufferer.

13

What Dose Makes the Poison?

It's a long-held medical maxim that the dose makes the poison. And to an overwhelming extent this is most certainly true. There are very few chemicals or substances that are not toxic in some amount. It's how much of a given substance we encounter that determines how dangerous that substance will be to us.

For example, during the 18th century, a pale complexion was considered attractive and a sign of good breeding. Tanning salons were definitely out and ghostly pallor was in. To achieve this well-bleached look, the members of King Louis XVI's court took arsenic, perhaps weekly. Although we consider arsenic to be highly toxic, neither King Louis nor his wife, Marie Antoinette, died of arsenic poisoning. In fact, some level of arsenic in the diet is still considered necessary for good health!

In contrast, many beneficial chemicals have caused death. Aspirin, one of the safest and most versatile medicines known, poisoned countless children before packaging laws were enacted, and, as we just noted in the previous chapter, analgesics as a category are today the number one cause of household poisonings in the US.[1] Similarly, table salt is a common and necessary part of our daily diet, yet if an adult ingested half a cup at once, the effect could be fatal.

Clearly it's quantity that makes a chemical a poison. But what quantity? The answer for every chemical is different and must involve two clear and distinct standards: one for acute toxicity and one for chronic toxicity.

Acute toxicity is measured by a statistical standard known as Lethal Dose (LD), which uses a benchmark called the LD50. The LD50 is the quantity of a chemical needed to kill 50 percent of the animals (usually mice or rats) in a test group. Because larger animals require larger doses of a chemical to exhibit toxic effects (i.e., it takes more arsenic to kill an elephant than a mouse), the LD50 is measured as the weight of chemical in milligrams (or mg) per kilogram (or kg) of animal weight needed to cause death.

For example, the LD50 of arsenic trioxide (a common form of arsenic), when measured in rats, is 15 mg/kg. This means about 15 mg (approximately one half of one-thousandth of an ounce, or 0.0005 ounces) would be needed to kill a one-kilogram (2.2-pound) rat. By comparison, 3,000 mg (approximately a tenth of an ounce, or 0.1 ounce) would be needed to kill a 200-kg (440-pound) gorilla.

Measuring acute toxicity is relatively simple. Of more concern, however, is the measurement of *chronic toxicity*, and that, as we've discussed, is an all but impossible proposition. That's because the human body is an unfathomably complex natural system whose thousands of parts interact in a variety of subtly different ways to create each unique individual. No two people are exactly alike and neither, therefore, are the ways each of our bodies responds to chronic household chemical exposures. A low exposure to a particular chemical that produces little or no negative health consequences in one person may have quite the opposite effect on another.

≈ A low exposure to a particular chemical that produces little or no negative health consequences in one person may have quite the opposite effect on another. ≈

Most of us, for example, think nothing of eating peanuts or products made with peanut-derived ingredients. Yet approximately 1.5 million Americans are allergic to this common legume, some dangerously so. Some 200 people die every year from severe reactions to peanuts, sometimes simply because they used a knife that had been wiped clean after making a peanut butter sandwich. Such wildly disparate exposure results between individuals make contact with household chemicals the equivalent of playing Russian roulette.[2]

When and if an illness does arise as a result of chronic exposure to a chemical, pinpointing that chemical and the chronic low-level dose that caused it is like trying to find a needle in a decades-old haystack of possibilities. As we've seen, the more time that passes between these causes and their ultimate effects, the harder it is to make a connection between them. Complicating the matter is the fact that the amount of a given chemical needed to produce a chronically toxic effect in a given individual often appears to be so small as to be well below any regulatory "safe dose" that may have been established for it. Hormone-disrupting chemicals are a key case in point. The amount of most hormone-mimicking chemicals required to create damage to the body's endocrine system can often be measured, as is the case with natural hormones themselves, in parts per trillion. Such levels are a million times lower than the far higher parts-per-million standards used in most chemical regulations to establish hazardous thresholds.

As just one example of this safety gap, the Environmental Working Group recently examined three common hormone-disrupting pollutants frequently found in human tissues. The chemicals, bisphenol A, atrazine, and methoxychlor were found to cause serious problems in animals at levels hundreds of times lower than those set as "safe" by current regulations. Lead is another case in point. Recent research into its effects on reading ability and test scores suggests that problems actually become greater at lower exposure levels.

The broad lesson here is that many pollutants are biologically active at very low levels and that safe exposure thresholds for chronic exposures need to be established just as they have been for acute exposures. Until these thresholds are established, we'll really have no idea how much exposure to what chemicals is harmful to our health over time.

≈ Many pollutants are biologically active at very low levels and safe exposure thresholds for chronic exposures need to be established. ≈

A Quick Look at Material Safety Data Sheets

Those who make and work with chemicals will be familiar with documents known as Material Safety Data Sheets, or MSDSs. An MSDS is a chemical information summary sheet whose use in manufacturing and commercial settings is required by the Occupational Safety and Health Administration (OSHA). These standardized forms provide varying degrees of additional data about the chemicals, products, or formulas used by a specific facility or in a specific product. They must be prepared for the employees of any company that handles the chemicals or products in question so that workers can better understand the hazards associated with the materials with which they're working. While companies are not legally required to provide MSDS information on their products to consumers, some will send copies upon request. Libraries of MSDSs can also be found online (See Resources).

Although having the additional information an MSDS provides can sometimes be helpful, MSDSs suffer from a number of serious faults that greatly diminish their usefulness. Should you decide to seek them for the products you use, a few caveats are in order.

First, most MSDSs were not designed for consumer use. They tend to have a high degree of technical orientation and decoding the information they contain can be a daunting process. Indeed, studies have shown that even workers who use MSDSs do not fully understand their contents.

Secondly, and more importantly, when it comes to MSDSs for products that are made from a combination of chemicals, the law requires that only those hazardous ingredients present in levels above one percent (or one-tenth of one percent for carcinogens, neurotoxins, and teratogens — chemicals capable of affecting fetuses) need be disclosed even though many chemicals present a clear danger to users when present in lesser amounts. In addition, OSHA regulations say that MSDSs need only list materials that meet the agency's official definition of hazardous[1] and are "known to be present in the workplace in such a manner that employees may be exposed under normal conditions of use or in a foreseeable emergency." If a chemical has not yet been studied and formally placed on OSHA lists of known hazardous materials, it does not need to have an MSDS created for it or be mentioned on any sheets for any products that contain it. That's a pretty big loophole through which many dangerous compounds can and do slip.[2]

This already limited disclosure is in many cases further restricted by rules which allow manufacturers to withhold certain information they consider to be a trade secret. In the simplest terms, if a manufacturer uses what they feel is a proprietary (i.e., secret) formula for their product (and most do!), they don't have to disclose the usual detailed information about it on their MSDS and needn't reveal the presence of certain ingredients.

For these reasons, although they may represent the most complete and indeed only source of ingredient information, MSDSs usually do not provide a complete chemical profile of the product in question. Further, studies of MSDSs have shown that although they are required to outline all potential health effects of exposure to those chemicals whose presence they do reveal, many are remarkably incomplete in this regard as well. No wonder many environmental advocates caution consumers that MSDS can't be relied upon to provide all the information needed to assess a product's true safety.[3]

Household Chemicals and the World Outside

Though we've spent this chapter looking at the ways in which the chemicals in consumer products affect our health and our households, there's more to the picture than that. Indeed, the effects resulting from our use of these products ripple far outside our homes' walls.

Though our use of household chemicals may take place indoors, these substances invariably escape outside where they can cause a host of problems. Whether we spray a product into air that's then carried outside on a breeze, rinse a product down our drain that leads to a nearby river or a sewage treatment plant, or throw its remains out with the trash, a variety of environmental impacts are created near and far from the point of actual use. Here's a quick look at these effects.

Air Quality

The manufacture, use, and disposal (especially through incineration) of many common consumer products cause a variety of hazardous chemicals and compounds to be released into the atmosphere. These releases include direct introduction to the air via intentional spraying, evaporation of a product once applied, accidental releases created by fumes and spills, and pollution created during the manufacturing process. It may seem like little if any air pollution is being created when we use chemical products at home, and usually very little is. But when you add up all the releases from all of the products in all of the households around your town or region, the impact can be huge and the public health concerns significant. Just take a look at these figures from California:[1]

- According to the South Coast Air Quality Management District roughly 108 tons of smog-forming fumes are emitted from consumer chemical products every day in homes in Los Angeles, Orange, Riverside, and San Bernardino counties.

- The use of these consumer products releases about twice as many polluting hydro-carbons into the air as all of the SUVs and light trucks driven in California.

- Disinfectants such as Lysol, which are exempt from regulation, release seven tons of emissions throughout the state every day. About 90 percent of the contents of an aerosol can of deodorant, for example, are hydrocarbon chemical propellants. These propellants are precursors to ozone, a key component of smog. Consumer products send out nearly twice as many of these kinds of hydrocarbons as all of the SUVs and light trucks operating in California.

- By 2020, emissions from household products are projected to exceed tailpipe emissions as the Los Angeles region's number one cause of smog.

Water Impacts

Use of consumer chemical products can also pollute ground water, underground aquifers, and bodies of water as small as a pond and as big as the sea. This contamination can occur during consumer use, manufacturing, or when a given product is emptied or rinsed down a drain and into a public sewage system or private septic tank. For example, in a city of one million people, approximately 372 million tons of toilet bowl cleaner and 1,569 tons of liquid household cleaner are washed down drains each year.[2] Many water treatment facilities throughout the country are over 100 years old, predating the chemical revolution. These aging plants are simply unable to process these and many other modern chemicals.[3]

≈ By 2020, emissions from household products are projected to exceed tailpipe emissions as the Los Angeles region's number one cause of smog. ≈

How bad is the problem? A 2002 study by the US Geological Survey tested 139 streams in 30 states for levels of 95 different contaminants. Researchers found that all kinds of wastewater substances had successfully eluded standard sewage treatment and escaped into America's waterways. Among the compounds found in water samples were the painkillers acetaminophen and ibuprofen, prescription medicines for cardiac disorders and hypertension, caffeine, the insect repellent DEET, and a number of chemicals from household cleaners including detergents and disinfectants.[4]

Because many household chemicals are persistent, and because traditional treatment methods are unable to remove them from the wastewater stream, these compounds tend to remain in the waters into which they're introduced. Depending on the chemicals and the levels in question, this pollution can cause everything from reproductive and developmental problems in wildlife to massive fish kills to phosphate-triggered algae blooms.[5]

Land Impacts

Consumer chemical products also contribute to land-based environmental concerns. Gathering their raw materials, manufacturing the products themselves, and using and disposing of them depletes non-renewable natural resources like petroleum, causes deforestation, increases the loss of wildlife habitat, promotes endangered species extinctions, contaminates soil, and creates hazards like landfills and toxic waste sites.

Our reliance on petroleum to create most of the chemical products we use causes a host of environmental problems in and of itself. Petroleum pollutes the environment when we drill for it, when we transport it (oil spills into oceans average 15,000 tons a year[6]), and when we refine it (America's 158 refineries release 84 million pounds of toxic pollutants into our air and water each year).[7] Every time we use a petrochemical cleaning product, we contribute to this pollution. And we further deplete an important global resource whose supplies are expected to become scarce sometime within the next 50 years.

SECTION THREE

The Dirty Secrets of Household Cleaners

OF ALL THE TASKS THAT WE HAVE TO TACKLE during the course of the average week, there's probably no chore that elicits more moans and groans than housework. While the completed task may provide the pleasure of knowing that our homes are free of dust, grime, and clutter, getting there is about as much fun as a root canal.

Given all this, it's no wonder that we've come to rely on an ever-expanding array of cleaning products to make the job easier, nor is it a surprise that these products have created a roughly 17 billion dollar industry.[1] We all like to clean our homes with as little blood, sweat, and tears as possible, and manufacturers have risen to that challenge by providing us with all kinds of miraculous sprays, concentrated detergents, polishes, wipes, waxes, and other cleaning solutions.

The result is an arsenal of dirt- and stain-fighting weaponry filled with impressively powerful synthetic cleaning agents, grease cutters, anti-redeposition agents, bleaches, builders, enzymes, optical brighteners, and other fantastic technologies that work under more varied conditions, against more forms of dirt, in colder water, in less time, and with less elbow grease than ever before. In fact, these products work so well, it's all but impossible to imagine cleaning without them. Yet perhaps we should, because behind their cheerfully sparkling labels of crystal mountain streams and fields of wildflowers waving in the freshest breezes, all too many household cleaning products hide a dirty little secret: they're made from synthetic chemicals that are toxic to people and dangerous to use.

The Incredible Case of the Shrinking Label

We know what you're thinking — cleaning products can't be *that* bad. If they were, manufacturers would have to tell us. They'd be required to let us know right there on the product label just what their products were made from and exactly what might happen when we used them. And if a particular product was exceptionally hazardous, it simply wouldn't be allowed to be sold in the first place. Right?

Not really. While we wish these things were true, the fact is only the manufacturer knows for sure what's really in any given household cleaner. And in the vast majority of cases they're neither willing nor legally obligated to reveal what these ingredients are or what hazards they represent.

How could this be? The answer is simple: contrary to popular belief, full disclosure of all the chemical ingredients cleaning products contain and all the potential health problems they might cause is simply not required by federal law.

Cleaning products have been regulated by the Consumer Products Safety Commission (CPSC) since the introduction of the Federal Hazardous Substances Labeling Act (FHSLA) in 1960. According to this 40-year-old law, cleaning product labels must warn consumers about any "immediate" dangers (i.e., acute hazards) that may occur in the event a product is used incorrectly.

This required warning takes the form of the following "signal" words:

• **Danger** or **Poison** means that a few drops to one teaspoon of the product, if ingested, can be life threatening.

• **Warning** or **Caution** means ingesting one teaspoon to one cup can be life-threatening, or that the product can cause serious irritation or irreversible damage to the eyes or skin upon contact.

Cleaning products are also regulated under Title 16, Chapter II of the Code of Federal Regulations. Title 16 expanded the definition of the word "toxic" as it applies to cleaning products. This revised definition addresses chronic health effects and declares that any ingredient that is a confirmed or probable carcinogen, neurotoxin, or developmental or reproductive toxin must be considered "toxic" as well and subject to the same labeling regulations as ingredients that pose immediate acute hazards. A cleaning product that contains any ingredients that meet this expanded definition would also have to be labeled with a signal word.

In theory, this should go a long way toward informing and protecting consumers about many of the more serious dangers hiding in household cleaners. And it would — if not for a loophole that allows manufacturers to combine their warnings about different hazards into a single statement if that statement gives consumers all the information they need to deal safely with each individual danger.

In other words, if a single warning about a given product's toxicity can be worded so it applies to both the acute dangers and the chronic dangers, that one warning is all that's required. Thus, if you should avoid drinking a cleaner because one ingredient could cause sudden poisoning, and you should also avoid drinking it because another of its ingredients is carcinogenic, all the manufacturer has to say is "do not take internally." While such warnings certainly offer good advice under any circumstances, consumers are rarely if ever able to discern whether the health threat they refer to is the obvious acute risk or a more hidden chronic risk.

Because cleaning products tend to contain both kinds of hazards, and because their labels can usually get away with issuing a single warning that simply advises us of the presence of "toxic" ingredients, regardless of whether those ingredients are acutely or chronically toxic, we don't have any real way to tell what specific dangers a product poses. Technically speaking, products *are* warning us about chronic dangers where those dangers are known, but these warnings are vague, and they usually refer to an acute poisoning hazard as well. In the absence of more detailed information, this more obvious latter association is the one we logically tend to make.

If you think that's bad, consider this: an even bigger loophole in labeling laws means that in many cases cleaning products don't even have to do this much. According to current regulations, a manufacturer can use a substance known to be chronically hazardous but omit all warnings or references to it by claiming that any exposure to that substance resulting from the product's use would not be not large enough to trigger the toxic effect.

For example, say studies have determined that it would take eating ten milligrams of chemical X per kilogram of body weight every day for six months to induce cancer (or neurological, reproductive or developmental effects). The manufacturer of a product containing chemical X can and usually will argue that the risk of a consumer ingesting such a large amount through the use of that product is unlikely. (Remember we're talking about ingesting quantities of the pure substance alone, not quantities of the product that contains that substance in a vastly diluted amount.) They're able to make this argument because it's the manufacturers themselves who get to decide how much of chemical X people are typically exposed to when a product containing that chemical is used.

≈ If a single warning about a given product's toxicity can be worded so it applies to both the acute dangers and the chronic dangers, that one warning is all that's required. ≈

Wherever scientific studies have shown a chronic danger to exist in the case of a particular chemical, manufacturers are allowed to determine what level of exposure risk their products that contain that chemical present. For example, they're allowed to make their own estimates of how much of chemical X you are likely to absorb by using how much of their spray cleaner how many times per week for how much of your life. If this estimate falls below the threshold needed to trigger the toxic effect, the manufacturer is once again legally off the labeling requirement hook, and a product that contains a known chronic hazard can be declared safe and free of the need to address that hazard on its label.

Furthermore (as if more were needed!), manufacturers also are allowed to figure out how to take the animal studies that typically demonstrate chronic risks and apply them to human beings. So, for example, if chemical X has been found to be carcinogenic in a study using rats as its test subjects, the manufacturer gets to decide how those rat results translate to human beings.

Needless to say, all these estimates and extrapolations are subject to all kinds of guesswork. And it doesn't take a degree in human nature to guess whose side manufacturers are likely to err on when it's their calculations that will determine what has to go on (and what can be left off) their products' warning labels.

Adding insult to this potential injury, of course, is the fact that very few of the ingredients used in cleaning products have been subjected to the kinds of testing required to determine chronic exposure risks in the first place. In cases where there is no toxicity data, manufacturers simply claim that no risk has been proven and so no warning is necessary.

The result of all these loopholes is that cleaning product labels neither completely, concretely, nor realistically address the very real, very common perils that are found in the tiny amounts of chemical cleaners we naturally encounter in daily life both during and after cleaning. In the simplest practical terms, they're really only warning us about what would happen if, for example, we dunked our head in a bucket of a particular product, not what might happen when we breathe the product's fumes and absorb it through our skin on a regular basis over the course of many years, even though such exposures are quite capable of causing a wide variety of chronic effects.

The Federal Hazardous Substances Labeling Act also requires only that manufacturers list "the common or usual or chemical name of the hazardous substance, or of each component, which contributes substantially to its hazard." In other words, if an ingredient isn't connected to a product's acute or chronic hazards, it doesn't have to be listed on the label. And since nothing else needs to be listed on product labels, nothing else usually is. Manufacturers are legally permitted to withhold any and all information about the bulk of the different chemical compounds they use in their cleaners. These secret ingredients can include all kinds of substances from solvents, dispersal agents and carriers to preservatives, buffering agents, and "inert" ingredients. They hide in the products we use thanks to lobbying efforts and lax federal regulations that allow cleaning product companies to keep their product formulas confidential in the name of protecting trade secrets.

Numerous studies have revealed the seriousness of such incomplete cleaning product labels. In a recent study of household products, for example, the National Environmental Trust found that 85 percent of those tested contained hidden hazardous ingredients. The organization contracted an independent lab and used federally approved testing methods to analyze 40 different household products, including various kinds of make-up, hair styling gels, soaps, furniture finishing products, disinfecting sprays and cleaners, and kitchen, toilet, and all-purpose cleaners. Test results showed that 34 of the products contained toxic ether glycols, organic solvents, or phthalates even though no mention of any of these substances was made on any of the products' labels.[1] Similarly, a study of product warnings conducted by the New York Poison Control Center found that 85 percent were inadequate.[2]

Test- and Approval-Free For You and Me

Aside from product labels that don't list all their ingredients or meaningfully address their hidden hazards, household cleaners have one other secret their manufacturers would prefer you didn't know: they don't have to be independently tested for safety nor approved before being introduced and sold to an unsuspecting public.

Contrary to widespread belief, there's no law that requires cleaning product companies to submit their products to third parties for unbiased safety testing nor is federal approval of a product formula required before it can be sold. (Disinfectants and sanitizers are a notable exception; they are regulated by the EPA as pesticides and are subject to prior approval.) Regulators at agencies like the EPA and the Consumer Product Safety Commission play little or no role in reviewing test results and approving a cleaning product for sale in the US.[1] In place of strict product testing and government oversight is a system of largely voluntary standards in which manufacturers themselves are responsible for all initial assurances of their products' safety.[2] Cleaning product companies are legally free to sell almost any product with almost any ingredient and need little more than their own okay to bring it to market.

This situation is made even more troubling by the fact that very little is known about most of the chemicals made and used in the US today. According to a 1998 EPA report, 43 percent of all chemicals produced in annual amounts of over one million pounds have no basic toxicity data at all and 50 percent have nothing more than preliminary screening data. Only 7 percent of these "high production volume" chemicals have a complete set of screening level toxicity data.[3]

Instead of a precautionary look-before-you-leap approach, it's "shoot first and ask questions later" where cleaning products are concerned. In most cases, any hazards or health effects that are caused by exposure to a particular cleaner or ingredient only become known after people have used the product in question, gotten sick, and reported this fact to federal authorities who only then are permitted to take action. Unfortunately, by the time such complaints usually surface, the product or ingredient causing all the trouble has been in widespread use for months or even years.[4]

In short, our regulatory system calls upon federal agencies to be reactive instead of proactive. The underlying problem, of course, is that this system allows manufacturers to regulate themselves. Decisions about what risks a product may pose to public health (and what type of labeling and/or warning it should bear as a result) are largely left to the company that makes it. (This system stands in stark contrast to the European model in which manufacturers must submit product formulations to government regulators who then use independent analyses to assess any potential dangers.) The result is that consumers from coast to coast are using hundreds of common products every day whose safety has not been assured and whose hazards remain unknown.

Meet the Usual Suspects

So far in this section, we've been looking at where many household chemicals come from and what can happen when we use and come into contact with them. But what sort of chemicals are we talking about? Here's a look at some of the primary kinds you're likely to encounter in the course of daily life.

Surfactants

Surfactants are a modern kind of detergent that perform the functions traditionally handled by old-fashioned soap. Although we're simplifying the science here, a surfactant is essentially a molecule with two ends that are often referred to as a head and a tail. The head is attracted to and dissolves in water. The tail is attracted to and dissolves in oils and fats. Thus a surfactant molecule is able to form a "bridge" between the grease and dirt being cleaned and the water doing the work. This linking action allows the former to dissolve into the latter. It literally makes oil and water mix and is the reason surfactants lie behind much of the actual cleaning accomplished by household cleaners.

Surfactants are classified in terms of their electrical molecular charge. Surfactants with a positive charge are called cationic. Those with a negative charge are called anionic. And those with no charge at all are called nonionic. Pure soap is an anionic surfactant. It's made by combining natural fats with lye in a reactive process called saponification, and it has all but disappeared from modern store shelves. This is because it tends to become less effective in hard water and can leave films behind. Modern chemical surfactants have risen to takes its place. And that's where the trouble starts, because many of these new surfactants are largely made from petroleum.

Petroleum-based surfactants are an ideal product from a purely performance perspective. They're cheap to produce, leave little or no film behind, and aren't easily defeated by hard water.

In the environment, however, pure petroleum-based surfactants are less than desirable. Because of their molecular structure, many are persistent and can remain for a long time in the soils and waterways into which they are discharged. This persistence is a problem because some surfactants have the ability to cause hormonal disruption and other illnesses in animals and people.

≈ **Vegetable-based surfactants are a clear step in the right direction from an environmental standpoint.** ≈

Vegetable-based surfactants, on the other hand, are a clear step in the right direction from an environmental standpoint. But most vegetable-based surfactants are modified with a small amount of petroleum material to increase their effectiveness.

You'll find surfactants in almost every kind of cleaning product because, after all, they're the primary ingredient responsible for doing the actually cleaning. Products that contain surfactants include:

- laundry detergents
- dishwasher detergents
- dishwashing liquids
- all-purpose and hard surface cleaners
- window cleaners
- toilet bowl cleaners
- bath and shower cleaners
- floor cleaners
- carpet and upholstery cleaners.

Solvents

Solvents are chemicals used to dissolve or disperse other materials, especially fats, oils, and greases. They have a unique and useful ability to quickly remove nearly everything, from the gunk left behind by a misplaced peel-and-stick label to oven grime, oily engine goo, and paint materials that otherwise aren't going anywhere. Solvents are often called degreasers, and there are hundreds of different kinds that are used in over 30,000 commercial combinations.

Degreasing products aren't the only place you'll find solvents hiding. Their innate ability to dissolve other substances makes them ideal elements in many kinds of consumer products where they act to keep other ingredients suspended and dispersed. When a solvent is used in this way, it prevents the other ingredients from clumping together. The result is a product that dispenses easily and maintains its original balance of ingredients from the first squirt to the last.

Most solvents are highly volatile, which means they evaporate easily. (Most solvents are classified as volatile organic compounds. See below.) For this reason, many household product formulas use them to help speed drying time when those products are used. Unlike water, which won't mix well with many chemicals and dries more slowly, solvents help create products that are easier to apply and more efficient to use.

Solvents, as a general rule, are among the most toxic components of a typical product formula. In addition to being severe eye, skin, and mucous membrane irritants, the majority of solvents can damage the neurological system, the liver, the blood, the lungs, and the kidneys. Most solvent exposures occur when their volatile vapors are inhaled, and even very short contacts can lead to negative health effects.

Unfortunately, solvents remain largely hidden in product formulas and their presence often cannot be directly confirmed by reading labels. However, we do know that the following types of products typically contain solvents and should generally be replaced with non-toxic alternatives:

- oven cleaner
- paint removers and strippers
- degreasers
- all-purpose cleaners
- furniture, floor, and metal polishes
- glass cleaners
- spot removers
- air fresheners and odor removers.

Volatile Organic Compounds

Volatile organic compounds, (VOCs) are carbon-based chemicals that form vapors at room temperature. Like solvents (most of which can also be classified as VOCs), they are easily evaporated into our homes' air. VOC fumes come from two predominant sources: the release of toxic gases from synthetic materials like foams and plastics (this is called outgassing or off-gassing) and the use of toxic cleaning products and other household chemicals.

There are hundreds of VOCs capable of causing everything from neurological and organ damage to cancer. Interestingly, many victims of multiple chemical sensitivities think their troubles began with an exposure to VOCs. Because of their high toxicity, VOCs are a major indoor air concern. (Readers should note that as is the case with other so-called organic chemicals like hydrocarbons, volatile organic compounds are labeled "organic" not because they're natural but simply because they contain carbon, the element upon which all organic life is based. This chemistry definition has nothing whatsoever to do with the more common consumer meaning of "organic," which denotes something made or grown without synthetic chemicals.)

As a general rule, when you can smell something, you're smelling a VOC. Fragrances, for example, are always composed of VOCs whether they're natural or synthetic. Similarly, the strong scents that come from many glass and surface cleaners are VOCs escaping from them in the form of gases.

Synthetic Dyes

Synthetic dyes are used to give products a pleasing color or alter an appearance deemed unappealing by the product's manufacturer. There are approximately 1,200 dyes used to color household products, the bulk of which are chemically derived from either petroleum or coal tars (a carcinogenic liquid or semi-liquid obtained from bituminous coal).[1] Coal tar colors can contain a variety of toxins, including benzene, xylene, napthalene, phenol, and creosol.[2] Synthetic dyes are often irritants. In addition, many are resistant to biodegradation and are highly toxic to aquatic life.

Synthetic Fragrances

Synthetic fragrances are added to products to make the things they're used on smell fresh or to cover up odors in the products themselves. They're added to formulas for purely aesthetic reasons and play no role in the actual function of the product. With the exception of natural cleaning products, virtually all scented household cleaners use artificial scents because they are far cheaper to produce. (Pound for pound, a natural scenting agent can cost as much as four thousand times its synthetic version.)[3] A recent government report targeted synthetic fragrances as one of the six categories of chemicals that should be given the highest priority for neurotoxicity testing along with insecticides, heavy metals, solvents, food additives, and air pollutants. Eighty-four percent of the ingredients used in fragrances have never been tested for human toxicity, or have had only minimal testing. In a list of 2,983 chemicals used by the fragrance industry, the National Institute of Occupational

Safety and Health (NIOSH) reported that 884 toxic substances were identified as capable of causing breathing difficulty, allergic reactions, multiple chemical sensitivities, and other serious maladies, including neurological damage. Key among these toxins are VOCs, which are the actively "smell-able" components of every fragrance, and phthalates, which are added because they help scents last longer.

The FDA has acknowledged that the incidence of adverse reactions to perfume products appears to be increasing and that these reactions involve the immune and neurological systems.[4]

Optical Brighteners

Optical brighteners are chemicals added primarily to laundry detergents to make fabrics seem brighter or whiter. These chemicals, which are engineered to remain behind once the product has been used, convert ultraviolet light into visible light. In this way, optical brighteners simply create an optical illusion. They coat the surface in question with fluorescent particles that act like mirrors and reflect visible light outward. (You can look for the presence of these particles by seeing if the cleaned item seems to glow unnaturally under a black light.) Surfaces treated with optical brighteners appear more effectively cleaned. Like fragrances, the optical brighteners responsible for this trick are added to products for reasons relating to perception, not performance.

≈ As a general rule, when you can smell something, you're smelling a VOC. ≈

Many optical brighteners are derived from benzene, a highly toxic compound. They don't readily break down in the environment, are toxic to fish, and can create bacterial mutations. In addition, these chemicals can cause allergic reactions when they come into contact with skin that is then exposed to sunlight. Many reports of "sunscreen failure" can be attributed to optical brighteners. When we dry off with a towel washed in a detergent that contained optical brighteners, some those brighteners are transferred to our skin. By applying a layer of sunscreen over these chemicals, we trap them there and a reaction can occur whose rash-like symptoms seem like sunburn to unsuspecting consumers.[5]

Inerts

Many household chemical products contain a large number of ingredients that are known as "inert ingredients." This classification, however, is highly misleading because these so-called inerts are quite often anything but. They're labeled "inert" not because they're harmless but simply because they're not technically considered an active ingredient involved in the marketed function of the product. (Household chemical products generally consist of active ingredients, i.e., the chemicals that actually do the work, and inert ingredients, a catch-all term for all the remaining "non-active" ingredients.)

Inert ingredients can include buffering agents, solvents, preservatives, dispersal agents and carriers, wetting agents, fillers, and other ingredients that help stabilize, dispense, and increase the potency, effectiveness, and ease-of-use of the product.

In the human body, inerts can be quite active. Of the approximately 1,400 chemicals the EPA allows manufacturers to call inert, 40 are known carcinogens and/or neurotoxins and 64 are believed to have the potential to cause these and other health effects.[6] At first glance, that seems like a small number until we understand that the vast majority of inerts have never been studied for their effects on our health. We simply don't know whether they're hazardous or not.

The Oops Factor

In addition to the ingredients they are supposed to contain, cleaners can be contaminated by hazardous foreign materials and substances during their manufacture. The sources of these contaminants include impurities present in the raw materials, the materials that are used in processing the product, or materials created as an unintended by-product when the original product is made. In addition, cleaning products can become contaminated by other chemicals or products produced in the same facility for the simple reason that most of these products are made in large manufacturing plants that produce a wide variety of compounds for an equally diverse number of consumer products.

In a 2004 analysis of chemical reporting data from New Jersey and Massachusetts for 364 product types (including non-consumer categories), the National Environmental Trust found that approximately 1.8 percent of the total amount of all chemical products shipped in those states consisted of substances that were there unintentionally. These materials, in the words of the report, "were simply along for the ride" in a total amount that exceeded 10 million pounds. Among them were large amounts of neurotoxins, carcinogens, and reproductive and developmental poisons.[7]

As just one specific example of the kinds of contamination that can occur, according to an internal EPA memo, a leading brand of household disinfectant spray was found at one point to have been contaminated by dioxins. Yet, according to the Office of Solid Waste and Emergency Response, the manufacturer "either failed to report contamination, substituted false information purporting to show no contamination or submitted samples to the government for analysis which had been specially prepared so that dioxin contamination did not exist .... (This) failure to report dioxin contamination of the disinfectant has prevented any ban or other alleviation of human exposures to dioxins in this product."[8]

Unpronounceably Unhealthy
A Look at Some of the Specific Chemicals in Your Cupboard

Incomplete labels make it impossible to know exactly what particular chemicals are in each specific cleaning product. Still, we can make some educated guesses about what ingredients different types of products are likely to contain based on lab analysis, manufacturer safety data sheets, published studies, and other resources. Here is a list of some common cleaning product ingredients, the kinds of products they're found in, and the health effects they're known to cause. While this will give you a general idea of the overall toxicity of the compounds many popular household cleaners contain, keep in mind that it barely scratches the surface. A complete list of all the chemicals used by the cleaning products industry would contain thousands of entries and require a whole book by itself.[1]

Chemical Name	Health Effects	Often Found In
Alkanol amines	Carcinogen precursors	All-purpose cleaners
Alkyl phenoxy ethanols	Hormone disruptors	Laundry detergents All-purpose cleaners
Amyl acetate	Neurotoxin	Furniture polishes
Butyl cellosolve	Liver/kidney neurotoxin	All purpose cleaners Window cleaners Spray cleaners Scouring powders
Sodium hypochlorite (chlorine bleach)	Severe irritant Carcinogen precursor	Bleaches Scouring powder Toilet bowl cleaners Disinfectants

Chemical Name	Health Effects	Often Found In
Cresol	Liver/kidney neurotoxin	Disinfectant products
Crystalline silica	Carcinogen	All-purpose cleaners Scouring powders
Dichloroisocyanurate	Reproductive, developmental, and immune system disruptor	Tub and tile cleaners Scouring powders Dishwasher detergents
Diethanolamines	Create carcinogenic nitrosamines	Detergents Dish liquids All-purpose cleaners
Dioxane	Immunosuppressant Carcinogen	Window cleaners Laundry liquids Dish liquids
Ethylene glycol	Neurotoxin	All-purpose cleaners
Formaldehyde	Carcinogen	Deodorizers Disinfectants Germicides
Glycol ethers	Reproductive toxin Liver/kidney neurotoxin	All-purpose cleaners Window cleaners Spray cleaners Scouring powders
Methylene chloride	Carcinogen Liver/kidney neurotoxin Cardiac trigger	Degreasers
Morpholine	Liver/kidney toxin	All-purpose cleaners Waxes Polishes
Napthalene	Kidney toxin Cataract trigger Carcinogen	Toilet cleaners Carpet cleaners Deodorizers
Nitrobenzene	Blood poison	Polishes
P-dichlorobenzene	Neurotoxin Hormonal disruptor Carcinogen	Deodorizers Mothballs
Phosphoric acid	Corrosive skin toxicant	Tub and tile cleaners Toilet cleaners
Phenol	Highly toxic general poison	Polishes Mold/Mildew cleaners
Stoddard Solvent	Neurotoxin	Degreasers Spot removers
Xylene	Reproductive/developmental toxin Neurotoxin, kidney toxin	Degreasers

Germ Warfare and Human Welfare
A Look at Antibacterial Products

Unless you've been hiding in a cave for the last decade, you've no doubt noticed the increasing presence of all kinds of antibacterial products on store shelves. Responding to consumers' rising fears about germs (or, in the opinion of some, perversely feeding these concerns), manufacturers have created a plethora of products from germ-proof soaps and cleaners to sanitizing pillows and even facial tissues.

While products like these may have a place in hospitals and certain homes, a growing chorus of medical and scientific experts believes that the recent explosion of antibacterial cleaning products is doing us more harm than good. The emerging opinion is that our efforts to rid our homes of all bacteria are probably weakening our bodies and creating virulent strains of dangerous germs resistant to all currently available controls.

To be sure, there are instances where the use of antibacterial products is appropriate. Households with newborn infants, elderly family members, and those with compromised immune systems can certainly use antibacterial products to their advantage. But most physicians and scientists feel that in the majority of homes antibacterials are not only unnecessary, they're unhealthy.

A new theory called the hygiene hypothesis says that it may not be such a great idea to live in a completely sterile environment. Researchers studying alarming rises in asthma, allergies, and other immune problems in the developed world now believe that our obsession with hyper-cleanliness may be a contributing factor. In essence, the hygiene hypothesis says that when we grow up and live in a germ-free environment, our immune systems don't get the workout they need to develop properly and stay in shape. In effect, with nothing to defend against, our body's defense systems get fat and lazy, and eventually become so soft that they're unable to respond effectively when hazardous germs and substances are final-ly encountered (as they inevitably will be). Because our immune systems naturally evolved in a dirty world, they're not only used to it they may even need it to stay sharp.

A recent study of European children living on farms, for example, found that those whose bedding contained the highest levels of endotoxin, a substance released by bacteria prevalent on farm animals and in farm soils, had the lowest rates of allergies and asthma.[1] Another study found that mice who had contact with a bacteria called Mycoplasma pneumoniae early in life had fewer allergic reactions than mice who hadn't had the bacterial contact.[2]

Studies like these suggest that living with germs has a vaccination-like effect, and that's an important finding in these antibacterial times. It's why experts suggest reserving the use of antibacterial products only for those rare instances when they're truly necessary.

≈ Antibacterial cleaners are the only category of cleaning product regulated by the EPA, which classifies their active ingredients as pesticides. ≈

That's getting increasingly harder to do because more and more products are being made with antibacterial ingredients. One recent study found that 76 percent of all liquid soaps and 29 percent of all bar soaps being sold in the US were anti-bacterial. That's 45 percent of all soaps on the market.[3] Yet the use of all these soaps is having lit-tle or no impact on sanitation or disease rates. According to a study at Columbia University, of New York City households with at least one preschooler present, there was no significant difference in the number of infections between households that used antibacterial soaps and detergents, and those that didn't.[4]

Perhaps the best way to understand the true nature of antibac-terial products is to think of them as pesticides for the body. In many ways, this is the most accurate description. After all, antibacterial compounds are designed for one single purpose: to kill living things. This point is under-scored by a simple fact: antibacterial cleaners are the only category of cleaning product regulated by the EPA, which classifies their active ingredients as pesticides.

Just as repeated exposure to some pesticides can cause certain insects to evolve a resist-ance to them, antibacterials may be causing bacteria to evolve into highly resistant, dan-gerous new strains. This brings us to our second antibacterial lesson: know your ingredients, because where bacterial resistance is concerned not all are created equal.

Antibacterial ingredients fall into two broad categories: general and specific biocides. General biocides disrupt so many cellular functions at once that the bacteria cell simply can't survive. Specific biocides, on the other hand, are like antibiotic medicines. They kill bacteria by targeting and interfering with very specific cellular functions. Specific biocides are troubling for the same reason as the antibiotics whose strategies they mimic: bacteria can evolve in their presence and become resistant to them. The result is what some experts call a "super-bug," a strain of bacteria that's developed an ability to survive an attack by substances like drugs and disinfectants. When these kinds of bacteria emerge, the stockpile of materials we count on to protect us from microbial hazards is rendered useless, and, from a public health perspective, we've plunged ourselves back to the dark ages.

There are also environmental factors to consider. Antibacterial chemicals can involve the use of toxins in their production or create toxic hazards when used. Many also persist in the environment where they accumulate in fish and other living things. Inside the home, they can leave hazardous residues behind on household surfaces, which can then be ingested by unsuspecting infants and others who touch these surfaces and then put their fingers to their mouths. With all these factors in mind, here's a look at common antibacterial ingredients:

- **Triclosan** is perhaps the most ubiquitous consumer antibacterial. It was once thought to be a general biocide. But scientists now believe it likely kills bacteria by affecting a specific enzyme in their cell walls, a method that could cause bacteria encountering triclosan to mutate into new resistant strains. Triclosan is also chemically related to the family of chlorinated compounds that includes dioxins, one of the deadliest classes of pollutant ever created. Under certain production conditions, dioxins can be created when triclosan is made, and when that happens, batches of this antibacterial and any products made from them become contaminated.
Similarly, researchers at the University of Minnesota have discovered that when triclosan is dissolved into water it can be converted by sunlight into a type of dioxin.[5] Though it would seem that this phenomenon should be quite rare, the conversion of triclosan into dioxin is probably happening in far more places than we think. The US Geological Survey recently tested the water from 139 streams in 30 states and found that triclosan contaminated a hefty 57 percent of all surveyed sites.[6] These findings showed that triclosan readily survives conventional wastewater treatment methods. As Americans rinse this common antibacterial down their drains while bathing and cleaning, large quantities appear to be entering the environment, where sunlight is able to change it into something far worse.
As a relatively new compound, triclosan remains largely unstudied. However, this chemical is believed to be a toxicant of the immune system as well as of human sense organs. The Environmental Defense Fund has given this chemical an Ecological Risk Score of 7 on a 1-10 scale where 10 is the most potentially hazardous.[7]

- **Triclocarban** is chemically similar to triclosan. Although studies have yet to identify how it kills bacteria, its resemblance to triclosan makes it suspect.

- **Benzalkonium chloride** is an ingredient in a family of antibacterial chemicals called quaternary ammonium compounds, or "quats." Although quats are a relatively safe type of general biocide, their manufacture involves the use of benzylchloride (a lung irritant), methyl chloride (a suspected carcinogen), and toxic chloroparaffins, a class of chlorinated hydrocarbons. Quats are also toxic to aquatic life and slow to biodegrade.

- **Sodium hypochlorite**, or **chlorine bleach**, is a general biocide. It's a toxic chemical that can burn the eyes and skin, cause respiratory problems, and create toxic fumes when mixed with other cleaners. In addition to this basic toxicity, the use of chlorine leaves behind residues of chlorinated hydrocarbons, which contaminate surfaces and whatever touches them. It also creates a class of carcinogenic materials called trihalomethanes, including the suspected carcinogen chloroform, when it combines with organic material in the general environment. For these and other reasons, its use is discouraged.

- **Alcohols** (ethyl, methyl, isopropyl, etc.) are general biocides. Methyl alcohol is a poison that is moderately toxic when absorbed through the skin and highly toxic when ingested. These chemicals are also flammable and may cause respiratory irritation when inhaled.

- **Phenols** are general biocides. Most frequently found in pine disinfectants, phenols are toxic when ingested, inhaled, or absorbed. Concerns are also emerging that they may mimic estrogen and disrupt the body's hormonal balance. This point is especially troubling because phenols tend to persist in the environment and accumulate in living tissue.

- **Hydrogen peroxide** is a general biocide and a good antibacterial choice. Hydrogen peroxide breaks down into harmless water and oxygen as it is used. When applied in the home, no toxic residues are left behind, no dangerous fumes are created, and no environmental damage occurs.

- **Tea tree oil** is a natural substance from the needle-like leaves of the Australian tea tree. Like pine oil, grapefruit seed oil, and certain other natural oils, it has broad antibacterial, antifungal, antiviral, and deodorizing properties. This general biocide is well-suited for many applications. However, tea tree oil contains naturally-occurring phenolic compounds and may be irritating to some people. Though it may seem expensive, tea tree oil has been shown to be an effective antibacterial even when diluted 200 times.

21

Ten Key Ways to Read Labels and Avoid Toxic Products

In recent years, as public awareness of the problems with synthetic cleaning products has increased, a new breed of cleaning product manufacturer has come up with a better alternative. These companies have combined the traditional ingredients our ancestors used with a broad range of previously unavailable naturally based ingredients made possible by new technologies. The result is a brand new kind of cleaning product, one that's as effective as its chemical counterparts but presents none of their toxic dangers when used around the house.

Sadly, figuring out which products are really safe, natural, and (importantly!) effective can be a challenge. That's because many manufacturers make misleading claims about the environmental benefits of their products. The same public awareness that has led to the creation of legitimately healthier alternatives has also led to a phenomenon called *greenwashing*. Greenwashing occurs when manufacturers attempt to label a product "green" or "environmentally friendly" when in fact it's not much different from regular products of its kind.

You'll find a brand-by-brand guide to cleaning products in the back of this book that will provide you with a comparative analysis and point you to the very safest alternatives. In addition to that research, there's some important on-the-spot investigating that you can conduct in the aisles of your local store in order to evaluate the products you find there and make the healthiest possible purchasing decisions. Such efforts aren't always easy but given all that's at stake they are certainly among the most important actions we consumers can take for our families.

When shopping for cleaning products, inspect labels carefully and ask yourself the following questions:

1. If the label includes the notice: "Poison," "Warning," or "Danger" stop right there and avoid the product altogether. Note that many products can contain the word "Caution" without necessarily being toxic. For example, any product sold in a powder form will be a potential irritant if it ends up in your eyes. If you see "Caution" on the label, use your judgment and ask yourself this: Does it refer to serious chemical hazards hidden in the product, or is it simply a common sense precautionary statement based on the fact that even some natural ingredients can be harmful in large doses?

2. Are all ingredients listed clearly on the label along with a statement that notes that full ingredient disclosure has been made, or are only acutely hazardous or active ingredients listed? Look for complete listings and avoid products that offer only a partial listing.

3. Are all ingredients listed by specific name or are they hidden under broad categories like "surfactant," "dispersal agents," "inert ingredients," etc.? Don't buy a product that lists its ingredients by category. Choose alternatives that have all their ingredients clearly listed by name.

4. Does the product label provide you with information concerning the source of each of its ingredients in order to help you assess its safety? Look for products whose labels help explain these origins and provide the most complete information. Avoid products that are content to simply offer a chemical or ingredient name with no further explanation. If a company doesn't want to tell you where an ingredient comes from, there's probably a reason why.

≈ If the label includes the notice: "Poison," "Warning," or "Danger" stop right there and avoid the product altogether. ≈

5. Are there any ingredients listed on the label that appear to be synthetic in nature? This is a difficult point to ascertain because even natural ingredients have chemical names, and most of these names are fairly unintelligible to those of us without degrees in chemistry. Still, it's worth trying to decode chemical names on product labels because they can provide important hints about toxicity. Certain clues in the names of chemicals are a tip-off to a toxic formula. While our system isn't completely fool-proof, the presence of any of the following indicate a product that likely should be avoided:

• The presence of "chlor" in any part of any chemical name indicates a chlorinated chemical.

- Any ingredient ending in "-ene" like benzene, toulene, or xylene indicates the likely presence of a petroleum-based solvent. Note that sometimes these chemicals are called benzol, toluol, and xylol, which makes the ending "ol" another identifier.

- Petroleum distillates or naphthas.

- Any ingredient with "glycol" as part of its name, indicating a petroleum-based polyol or ether.

- Any ingredient with "phenol" as part of its name, especially at the end, indicating the use of toxic coal tar derivatives.

6. If a product says that it is biodegradable, what length of time is being referred to? If it isn't "readily biodegradable," then it may take several lifetimes to break down, which effectively makes its toxicity semi-permanent.

≈ The decision to stop using synthetic chemical cleaners is one of the most important ones you'll ever make for the health of your family and the safety of your home. ≈

7. Is there information on the label that says the product is either "combustible" or "flammable," or is there a warning statement that says the product should not be stored in temperatures above 120°? Such warnings usually indicate the presence of hazardous solvents, which typically account for the vast majority of the flammability hazards represented by cleaning products.

8. Is there a warning statement that says the product should not be used around flame or open fires? This is another clue to the presence of hazardous solvents.

9. Are there any precautionary statements on the label that warn of possible air quality dangers, such as a warning that the product needs to be used in a well ventilated room, that users should avoid breathing product vapors, or that the product can cause respiratory irritation and should be avoided by people with asthma, respiratory illnesses, emphysema, etc.? Avoid any products that have these or other similar statements.

10. Is there a precautionary statement on the label warning that the product can cause skin irritation? Avoid any products that have such a statement.

If you can't find the answers to these questions on cleaning product labels, you may be able to obtain them from the manufacturers. Most companies offer a toll-free phone number consumers can use to contact them and ask such questions directly. In addition, some manufacturers will send you a Materials Safety Data Sheet (MSDS) for their product if you request one. (See Chapter 14 for more on MSDSs.) Wise consumers will make good use of these services and understand that a company's refusal or inability to answer these important questions by providing further detailed information is grounds for refusal to purchase the product.

We think that the decision to stop using synthetic chemical cleaners is one of the most important ones you'll ever make for the health of your family and the safety of your home. When you decide to make the switch from toxic products to healthier alternatives, you'll need to make a clean sweep of your home looking for and removing the chemical cleaners and other products you find in your cabinets, closets, and storerooms. As you round up the offending suspects, please keep one very important thing in mind: the materials you're collecting for disposal may be extremely dangerous and classified as hazardous waste by environmental authorities. That's how dangerous they are!

Special disposal methods are needed to deal with these materials safely. Don't throw them out with your regular household garbage or dispose of them by pouring each bottle down the drain. Instead, take them to your local hazardous waste collection center. If your community doesn't have such a center, it may offer special hazardous waste collection days at certain times and places throughout the year. If you are unsure what programs exist where you live, call your state or local environmental, public health, hazardous waste, or solid waste agency; your local landfill; or your local poison control center. These authorities can tell you how to safely get rid of the toxins in your home in a way that won't affect the health of your family or your community.

22

Trouble in Paradise
The Challenges Natural Cleaning Products Face

Now that you've learned about traditional chemical cleaning products and mastered the art of reading their labels, you've no doubt found yourself running (and possibly even screaming!) straight into the arms of the many natural, non-toxic alternatives that have made their way in recent years from their original niche in health food stores to mainstream supermarkets. This relatively new breed of safer and healthier cleaning products promises to provide all the performance and none of the problems associated with its synthetic chemical counterparts. Made from ingredients that occur in nature, these cleaners seem to be everything petrochemical products are not: natural, non-toxic, biodegradable, and safe for children and other living things. In short, they appear to be just about perfect.

As we all know, however, there's no such thing as perfect. In the case of natural cleaners, some of these products aren't necessarily telling the whole truth about their ingredients, and some manufacturers are even engaged in the practice of greenwashing. For example, the popular product Simple Green, which from its name to its advertising is marketed as a safe, non-toxic alternative cleaner, contains the dangerous chemical butyl cellosolve, a compound found in traditional toxic cleaners like Formula 409 and Windex. But you wouldn't know it from reading the label.

Even those products whose labels do tell it straight and that represent the very best and healthiest available alternatives are not without their limitations and opportunities for improvement. Natural product development is an ongoing process, and honest companies will be open about this important point. (See Section 7 to find out which products you can trust.)

It's also a simple fact that ecological effects are created by all cleaning products, not just those made from toxic compounds. While natural formulas are clearly the very healthiest choice consumers can make, they are not immune to a basic fact of life: there is simply no such thing as a completely impact-free ingredient. Even the cleanest, purest, gentlest, safest ingredient is going to create some kind of impact on some facet of the environment at some point in its life cycle. The good news is that these impacts are nowhere near as serious as those created by toxic traditional products. Still, in the interests of a fully informed cleaning public, they are worth a brief discussion.

Natural and non-toxic cleaning products largely rely on surfactants derived from plant-based raw materials to accomplish their cleaning. The crops used most often for this purpose are corn, soybeans, and coconuts. (Other crops, notably citrus fruits, are also used in natural cleaners, but not to create surfactants.) These agricultural products create a variety of environmental and human health impacts before the raw materials they provide are even transformed into cleaning formula ingredients.

These impacts include pesticide use, the ecological effects of monoculture crops grown on huge factory farms, land use issues that center around the conversion of wild lands to farm lands, and, increasingly, the issue of genetically modified organisms (GMOs), which are plants that have had genetic material from other organisms added to their own DNA in order to attain certain characteristics like pesticide resistance, faster growth, hardier fruits, etc.

A discussion of the perils of genetic engineering is beyond the scope of our book, but suffice it to say that this new science presents myriad very serious potential problems. When a cleaning product uses raw materials obtained from GMO corn or soybeans, the two most commonly modified crops, it contributes to these problems.

Once a raw material leaves the farm, its impacts continue to accumulate. For starters, it has to actually leave the farm, which means it must be transported using fossil fuels, often over great distances, and fossil fuel use, of course, has a unique set of impacts all its own. At the factory, the crop must be processed in order to isolate the starches and oils that will be used as the basic building blocks of the desired surfactant. This step also requires energy. In addition, toxic solvents are sometimes used to extract the desired oils, instead of simple mechanical pressing. While these solvents are almost always captured for reuse, small quantities may escape into the desired oils. This solvent contamination is removed by subsequent processing, but this means the solvent escapes in small quantities into the environment, which is never a good scenario.

Once the final raw materials have been refined, they must be turned into surfactants. This is accomplished by combining the material with other ingredients. For example, vegetable oils combined with lye become soap. Coconut oil combined with sulphuric acid and lye turns into sodium lauryl sulfate, a common detergent. Many natural products use surfactants made from a class of compounds called alcohol ethoxylates, which are created by combining vegetable oils with a petroleum-derived chemical called ethylene oxide. This process is called ethoxylation. While they are one of the safest kinds of surfactants from a human health standpoint, alcohol ethoxylates do not come without a price. In addition to sustainability issues surrounding the use of a petroleum reaction agent, ethoxylation creates a by-product called 1,4-dioxane. Dioxane (not to be confused with dioxin, a much different toxin) is a weak carcinogen. Though this means it takes an appreciable quantity to create illness in laboratory tests, dioxane nonetheless represents a health hazard of some small degree. When created by ethoxylation, it remains behind in the finished product as a contaminant. To deal with this impurity, product manufacturers set targets for the amount of dioxane they are willing to tolerate in their otherwise pure and healthy surfactant. Many use the European Union safety standard of 20 parts per million (ppm), but others insist on dioxane levels no greater than 5 ppm.

An alternative to ethoxylated surfactants can be found in a class of surfactants called alkylpolyglucosides. Alkylpolyglucosides are made by combining raw materials from soy and/or palm kernels with ingredients obtained from corn. Because they are 100 percent naturally based and require no ethylene oxide in their production, alkylpolyglucosides are dioxane-free. But in a virtual case study that models some of the challenges natural product manufacturers face, these surfactants are found to be very expensive to manufacture, and any cleaner using them would have to be priced so high as to be unaffordable and, by extension, quite unpopular. In addition, alkylpolyglucoside surfactants have a very thick texture that makes them extremely difficult to work with. While neither of these obstacles is insurmountable, they currently conspire to put this alternative out of reach as a practical surfactant alternative.

A substance called d-limonene is another ingredient frequently used in natural products. It's often hailed as a powerful natural cleaner and degreaser, and benefits from a strong orange scent, which consumers interpret as a sign of a safer product. D-limonene is found in citrus fruits and is a member of a family of plant kingdom chemicals called terpenes. Terpenes are extremely effective natural solvents, and d-limonene is no exception. Balanced against these performance abilities, however, is the fact that d-limonene is classified as a volatile organic compound (VOC), one that can combine with ozone to form smog and harm lungs if inhaled in sufficient quantity. D-Limonene is also a sensitizer, a compound that causes a substantial number of people repeatedly exposed to it to become allergic. So while d-limonene is a better solvent as far as the environment is concerned, it's not without its own adverse effects.

There is also the issue of preservatives in natural cleaning products. Most natural cleaners consist of water and vegetable oil-derived surfactants. From the perspective of the earth's many microbes, this is about as ideal a situation as they're likely to encounter. These microbes have, after all, evolved over millions if not billions of years to use vegetable oils as a food source and water as a medium for life. This biological history makes natural cleaners ripe for bacterial growth. On the one hand, this is a good thing. It means that the product is, in fact, quite natural. But on the other hand, no one wants to open their all-purpose cleaner and find a slimy clump of bacteria living inside, however harmless it might be. To prevent this kind of unhappy surprise, manufacturers add various preservatives to their products. At this stage in the development of natural cleaners, these preservatives must be made from petrochemicals. This is because natural preservatives, many of which are also used in the preservation of food, work only in products with a neutral or acidic pH value. They do not perform well or at all in products with an alkali pH, which most cleaning products tend to have. The challenge is to find those petroleum-based preservatives with the lowest possible toxicity to people and the environment. We're happy to report that a few exist which are relatively low in toxicity to humans and wildlife, and quick to biodegrade. These preservatives are better choices than natural compounds like ethanol, which is also a VOC, parabens, or potassium sorbate, all of which are effective only in neutral or acidic conditions. However, all petroleum-based preservatives have the fundamental problem of being made from crude oil, and the environmental costs of extracting, transporting, and refining this raw material will always be high.

≈ Knowing that everything leaves a footprint on the earth, the object of the game is to choose and use those ingredients that leave the smallest mark possible so that consumers can do the same. ≈

And that's the lesson to be learned: even though a material may be natural or mostly natural, it's not necessarily impact-free. Indeed, in a certain respect, all of nature is really just a giant chemical factory. It is an amazing, mysterious, beautiful, profound, and even sacred chemical factory to be sure, but a chemical factory nonetheless. (Even we human beings are, from a strictly biological standpoint, little more than ambulatory bundles of chemical reactions.) Those chemicals may be natural. They may be environmentally safe in their particular context. They may be the best choices for the products we use. They may even exist inside us. But they are still chemicals, and just like petrochemicals, they can be associated with hazards both anticipated and unforeseen.

The purpose here is not to engender frustration or dissatisfaction with natural products, only to offer the important reminder that there's no such thing as a free lunch. Everything has a price. Nothing is perfect. But some things are closer to being perfect than others. Vegetable-based surfactants will always be far better for both the earth and the people who use them than petroleum-derived surfactants. D-limonene is a much better choice than butyl cellosolv, a common toxic solvent. Some synthetic preservatives, counterintuitively, are better choices than natural ones. In deciding which of these and other kinds of ingredients to use in their formulas, natural product companies engage in the art of the trade-off. Theirs is a balancing act in which the ingredient with the lowest impacts where it really counts wins. Knowing that everything leaves a footprint on the earth, the object of the game is to choose and use those ingredients that leave the smallest mark possible so that consumers can do the same. A fair and complete discussion of the issues relating to cleaners, other chemical products, and their alternatives can't be had without this essential knowledge.

If you're feeling a bit disappointed or even a tad ripped off by this news, don't be. Natural, non-toxic cleaner alternatives have only been around for a short time. They simply haven't had much of a chance to evolve, and any chemist involved in their creation will tell you that as the natural cleaning field continues to grow, the chemistry and availability of natural surfactants will only continue to improve.

Consumers, in fact, have a lot to look forward to. What kinds of things are on the horizon? Developments that someday will likely become a reality include the use of organically-based, non-GMO raw materials, the creation of toxin-free surfactants using 100 percent natural raw materials, and the discovery of naturally-based preservatives. In a nutshell, all the shortcomings we've discussed here will be solved, and that will make natural cleaners an even better choice than the excellent alternative they already are today.

A Better, Healthier Way to Clean

LET'S SUM UP OUR STORY thus far: traditional chemical cleaning products are largely unregulated and untested. They contain an extraordinary variety of toxic ingredients. Exposure to these chemicals can cause all kinds of unpleasant health effects. Yet for the most part these ingredients aren't disclosed on product labels. We usually have no way to tell what's really inside the products we use or what might happen when we come into contact with the hidden hazards these all too secret formulas contain.

So ... just what the heck are we supposed to do? No one wants to return to the exhausting days of endless housecleaning toil. Nobody wants to come home to a castle that's anything less than clean. On the other hand, it's abundantly clear that the modern cleaners we've been relying on to make short work of all our housework are dangerous at best and downright deadly at worst. Where exactly does that leave us?

The answer is simple: in the hands of Mother Nature.

23

Recipe For Safety
Making Your Own Household Cleaners

Once upon a time, things were different in America's cleaning cupboards. In the days before the chemical revolution of the 20th century, our ancestors relied on naturally occurring materials and substances to help them with the housework. These included things like pure vegetable soaps, grease-cutting vinegars, abrasives like calcium carbonate and baking soda, citrus oils to remove odors and grime, and essential oils of plants like birch and lavender to sanitize surfaces in the home.

Not only did these homemade concoctions work well in many circumstances, they had the additional advantages of being inexpensive to make and completely non-toxic to use. For these reasons, many people are happily rediscovering the art and science of do-it-yourself cleaning products and creating much healthier homes in the process.

The biggest surprise people have when they decide to make their own cleaners is how many they can make from so few ingredients. Indeed, an almost endless variety of safe homemade substitutes for toxic chemical cleaning formulas of all kinds can be easily prepared from just a handful of common natural materials.

With these items in hand, you can make almost any kind of formula and clean almost anything. Keep in mind as you go that though these ingredients are natural, they clean because they're powerful. The compounds they contain, while natural and biodegradable, are still chemically active and should be used with a healthy amount of respect. In addition, some readers may find that certain natural oils are irritating, and therefore personally unsuitable for use.

An excellent recipe-filled resource for learning more about making and using your own natural cleaners is the book *Better Basics for the Home* by natural household formula expert Annie Berthold-Bond (see Resources). This volume is highly recommended to anyone who wishes to take non-toxic cleaning into his or her own hands. It will show you how to take the following basic ingredients and transform them into amazing sprays, cleansers, waxes, polishes, and more. For the short term, we've included some sample recipes in the following pages that will help you harness the inherent cleaning power of these safe and natural materials.

Here are the core ingredients your natural cleaning cupboard should contain.

INGREDIENT	PURPOSE
Baking Soda	Deodorizer, non-abrasive scouring powder
Beeswax	Floor and furniture wax
Borax	Deodorizer, non-abrasive scouring powder, all-purpose cleaner, mold inhibitor, rust stain remover
Carnauba wax	Wood floor and furniture wax
Citrus fruit like orange, lemon and lime	Grease cutter, deodorizer, flea repellent
Eucalyptus oil	Insect repellent
Favorite essential oils	Air freshening, scenting homemade formulas
Hydrogen peroxide	Bleaching agent and antibacterial
Jojoba oil	Wood polisher
Lavender oil	Disinfectant, deodorizer
Natural vegetable-based liquid soap (like Dr. Bronner's)	General detergent product substitute
Neem tree oil	Insect repellent
Olive oil	Wood polisher
Washing Soda (sodium carbonate)	Grease- and grime-cutter, wax remover, deodorizer
White Distilled Vinegar	Dissolving hard water mineral scale and greasy build-up, removing tarnish, cleansing wood and glass
Tea Tree Oil	Antibacterial, antifungal, and antiviral agent; deodorizer
Toothpaste	Metal polish

24

Coming Clean In the Kitchen, Part One
Lovin' Your Oven and Caring for Your Counters

For vast numbers of Americans, the kitchen is the center of the home. Drawn by the many rituals of eating and drinking, the delicious smells of cooking food, and its function as a nerve center of sorts, we tend to gravitate toward the kitchen as the spot where friends and families most often come together for gatherings both spontaneous and planned.

Our kitchens provide our physical sustenance and fulfill our emotional needs. But the same place where we cook, eat, and assemble is often inadvertently one of the most toxic spots in the modern house. Ironically, this is because we seek to keep our kitchens cleaner and safer than almost anywhere else in the house. After all, this is where all our food is and no one wants to store, prepare or consume their meals in anything less than an optimum germ-free environment.

Yet as we all know from personal experience, maintaining a sparkling clean kitchen means confronting some of the more vexing cleaning dilemmas. From baked-on oven grease and heavily trafficked floors to bacteria left behind by raw meats and that leftover lasagna-turned-science-experiment you forgot was in the back of the fridge, kitchens present us with an almost constant onslaught of challenges. To meet them, we often turn to all kinds of tough chemical cleaners, scorched-earth disinfectants, and industrial-strength grime-fighters. But our use of these materials has the unintended side effect of transforming our kitchens into hazardous waste sites, the very last thing we want or would expect to happen.

A prime cause of the chemical trouble that often boils over in our kitchens is all the grease they accumulate. In the course of cooking, oils and grease get spread from countertops to oven floors. To remove them, we rely on a variety of chemical cleaners. Some, like all-purpose cleaners, we spray and wipe. Others, like oven cleaners, we leave in place for extended periods of time in order to allow them to eat away at stubborn baked-on, caked-on grime.

In general, these kinds of formulas rely on two different types of chemical compound to do their dirty work. First, a solvent is used to dissolve the grease or oil and lift it from the surface in question. (See page 55 for more on these materials.) Then a surfactant (see page 56) is usually employed to mix the now-lifted grime with water and allow it to be easily and completely wiped away. In the case of oven cleaners, dangerous acids like lye may also be included in the formula to help eat away at hardened deposits. It's because of ingredients like these that oven cleaners are often the most toxic cleaning product found in a typical home. Using these products contaminates kitchen surfaces with chemical residues and exposes us to hazardous fumes.

Fortunately, there are a number of effective natural ingredient alternatives waiting on store shelves. These products use a variety of compounds obtained from plants and other healthier sources to do the work performed by the synthetic surfactants, solvents, acids, and other petrochemicals found in traditional cleaners. Citrus fruits, for example, provide safe grease-cutting compounds that make short work of oily grime. Hydrogen peroxide, a non-toxic agent that breaks down into water and oxygen, sanitizes surfaces. Vegetable-derived soaps and surfactants clean up dirt and soils effortlessly.

Another option is to make your own cleaners using natural ingredients. In *Better Basics for the Home,* natural household formula expert Annie Berthold-Bond offers the following homemade alternatives:

Heavy Duty All-Purpose Counter Cleaner
Ingredients:

2 teaspoons washing soda	1/2 teaspoon natural liquid soap
2 teaspoons borax	1 cup hot water

Mix these ingredients in a spray bottle, shake well, and spray. Note that surfaces must be wiped thoroughly or a safe but unsightly whitish residue will be left behind by the washing soda. This formula will keep indefinitely for use over time.

Oven Cleaner

Believe it or not, Ms. Berthold-Bond swears by a safe and simple combination of baking soda and water for cleaning even the toughest, most baked-on oven messes. Just sprinkle baking soda in the bottom of the oven until it completely covers all offending matter, spray it with water until very damp, re-wet occasionally, and then let it sit overnight. In the morning, grease and grime will be easily wiped away.

25

Coming Clean In the Kitchen, Part Two
The Dish on Your Dishwasher

A critical epicenter of activity in our kitchens is the dishwasher. Fifty-one percent of all American homes have one of these time- and labor-saving devices, yet it surprises many to learn that they're the most toxic appliance in the modern home.

Over the course of approximately 30 experiments, researchers at the EPA and the University of Texas recently documented the dishwasher's role as a leading cause of indoor air pollution. Pollutants released by dishwashers include the chlorine added to both public water supplies and dishwasher detergents, volatile organic compounds like chloroform, radioactive radon naturally present in some water sources, and other volatile contaminants that have worked their way into public water supplies. When these materials are exposed to the piping hot water that circulates through your dishwasher as it cleans, they are easily "stripped out" and evaporated into the air.

Depending on the material in question and your water temperature, dishwashers can reach 100 percent efficiency when it comes to transferring water pollutants and detergent chemicals to indoor air. Because these machines vent about six liters of air per minute into your home as they work, they're continuously releasing any water-borne toxins throughout each operating cycle. Even more problematically, the air pollution created by routine venting is often exceeded by the single large burst of contaminated steam that's released whenever a dishwasher is opened before its contents have cooled.

Although it certainly sounds a little odd to say, protecting yourself from your dishwasher means taking steps like these:

- Use a chlorine-free dishwasher detergent. This will greatly reduce the burden of chlorine and other chemicals in its water, which in turn reduces your exposure to them.

- Ventilate your kitchen during and after dishwasher operation. This can mean opening windows, running your stove's ventilation fan (assuming it vents outside and not back into your kitchen), and using window fans.

- If you're connected to a public water system that's using chlorine to treat drinking water, filter your home's water supply. An activated carbon filter placed where water enters your home will remove chlorine and most volatile chemicals. It will also filter water used in your washing machine and shower — two other hot-water sources of chlorine fumes.

- Have your water tested for radon. If results are positive seek solutions from radon abatement professionals.

- Keep your dishwasher closed and sealed for at least an hour following a completed cleaning cycle. This will prevent the hot burst of pollutant-laden steam that escapes when dishwashers are opened immediately following their use.

- If you have a "no dry heat" option on your dishwasher, use it. This prevents the activation of its heating coils. These coils heat up the inside of your dishwasher and quickly evaporate the final rinse water, which allows that water to transfer its toxic load to indoor air. Deactivating the heated dry cycle also saves energy.

- Only run your dishwasher when it's completely full. Running a dishwasher when it's less than full means you're using it more often than necessary and increasing its contributions to unhealthy indoor air. And it means you're using more water and energy than needed.

- Make sure your detergent is phosphate-free, too. Contrary to popular belief, phosphate use is still legally permitted in dishwasher detergents, and phosphates may constitute as much as 20 percent of a product's formula.[1] (Dishwasher detergents contain levels of phosphorus as high as 8 percent, which translates to a phosphate level of 20 percent.) Once phosphates are discharged into the environment they promote massive algae growth in local waters. These sudden blooms of algae trigger a process called eutrophication in which local waters become starved of oxygen and devoid of life. This issue is of special concern to anyone living near a lake or pond.

Coming Clean In the Kitchen, Part Three
Battling Food-Borne Bacteria

Kitchens are also the main source of our exposure to dangerous bacteria in the home. Infamous interlopers like Salmonella and *e. coli* travel on everything from meat to produce, and once loosed in our kitchen they can contaminate food, utensils, and surfaces, and make us sick.

Preventing these microbial hazards and keeping your kitchen healthy is simply a matter of practicing common sense precaution when handling raw foods. Here are some tips to help you safely handle and prepare raw foods:

- Keep your cutting boards clean. While there's some controversy about whether wood or plastic cutting boards are safer in terms of their potential to hide harmful bacteria (studies exist in support of both sides of this argument), thorough cleaning makes the debate moot. Whichever kind you choose to use, scrub your cutting board well with soap and hot water after each use, and treat it to a generous five-minute soaking in a 1:5 solution of vinegar and water before storing. Never cut produce on a board you've cut meat on without first washing and treating it. Better still, maintain separate cutting boards for meats and produce.

- Similarly, wash all your knives carefully between each use. Never use a knife on produce that you just used on meat without first subjecting it to a thorough washing. An even better idea is to assign each knife you'll be using to either meat or produce use and then stick with that system throughout that meal's preparation.

- Human hands are a key way that bacteria get spread around the kitchen. Wash your hands frequently during all food preparation. After you've touched meat, don't touch anything else until you've washed. When it's time for the final cleanup, wash appliance door handles, cabinet knobs, and drawer pulls.

- Wash produce thoroughly as well. Remember: while meat is the most common source of bacterial contamination in the kitchen, produce is not immune. Vegetables can also be contaminated along the way from field to fridge, especially leafy greens, sprouts, mushrooms, and foods like broccoli, whose many nooks and crannies can easily protect and transport bacteria.

- Be mindful of where you prepare meat and what surfaces have had contact with it. Clean these areas and surfaces carefully immediately after that contact occurs. Try to restrict your handling of raw meat to a single confined area and do all meat-related prep at once in order to isolate these activities. Keep your eyes peeled for the potential for cross-contamination and head these occasions off before they occur.

- Don't use a cloth or sponge to wipe up after handling meat. These reusable materials will trap bacteria and then spread them to previously uncontaminated surfaces when they're used again. Instead, use recycled paper towels for cleaning meat prep areas and dispose of them immediately following use.

- Even if you haven't used them to clean up after meat preparation, sanitize your sponges by microwaving them for a least a minute at full power. As natural reservoirs of moisture that can often remain damp for days on end, sponges are a prime breeding ground for bacteria of all kinds that will then be spread around your kitchen as you use them to clean. Similarly, regularly launder dish cloths and towels that you use for cleaning.

- Don't serve food on kitchenware that's been used to prepare it. For example, a common mistake many make is to carry a platter of raw meat out to the grill and then use that same platter to carry this food back inside when it's cooked. Similarly, don't serve foods in any container that's been used to marinate them unless that container was also used to cook them.

If your kitchen experiences a burst of cooking activity that was difficult to control or monitor, or hosts an unusual abundance of potential microbe-carrying foods at one time, you may wish to perform general sanitization of all its surfaces when all is said and done. But be careful what you use to practice this hygiene! As we explained in Chapter 20, many antibacterial cleaners and related products aren't good for you or the environment. If you can't find an antibacterial product that uses safe hydrogen peroxide or non-toxic essential oils, you can safely sanitize surfaces by first wiping them clean with vinegar and then applying a spray cleaner with a three percent hydrogen peroxide solution, the concentration typically sold for home use. (Note that hydrogen peroxide is affected by exposure to light. If you choose to keep a preloaded spray bottle around the house, that bottle should block light and be stored in a dark place.)

Perfluorochemicals
The Stuff of Teflon® Is Sticking To Us

They are among the world's most recognizable brands; shining symbols of life-made-simpler by the modern miracles of space-age technology: Teflon, Stainmaster®, Scotchgard®, SilverStone®. When these brands are around, things don't stick, stains don't stain, and we don't have to scrub stuff nearly as much as we used to. Recent evidence, however, suggests that non-stick coatings like these may be freeing more than food and spilled grape juice. They may be letting loose the molecules they're made from and sticking with us for a very long time.

From cooking pans to the bedroom carpet, non-stick coatings, treatments and materials have become such an integral part of North American homes that they've entered our vernacular and become figures of speech. Ronald Reagan, for example, was christened the Teflon president because controversy seemed to bounce right off his administration. Similarly, reputed gangster John Gotti was called the Teflon Don because prosecutors could never get their charges to stick.

Whether it's Scotchgard or Silverstone, today's non-stick materials are based on a class of compounds called perfluorochemicals, or PFCs. PFCs have some unique properties that make them extremely useful. Resistant to chemicals and heat, virtually nothing sticks to or can be absorbed by PFCs or products made from them. These attributes make them ideal coatings for cookware, upholstery, food packaging, appliances, clothing and many other products, including floor wax and shampoos, which often contain PFCs because they have an innate ability to repel grease and oils.

The PFC family of chemicals consists of a variety of different substances. Chief among these is a compound called perfluorooctanoic acid, or PFOA, a key building block of many non-stick products. It also is created when other types of PFCs break down during use.

Over the years, researchers have discovered a number of unsettling things about PFOA. They've found that it does not biodegrade or break down in the environment. In this respect, PFOA is much like other notorious persistent chemicals, especially dioxins, PCBs, DDT, and related chlorinated compounds. However, there is one critical difference: Though chlorinated chemicals like dioxins are resistant to decomposition by the forces of biodegradation, they don't last forever. Depending on the particular compound in question, they may have half-lives of hundreds if not thousands of years, but nature *will* eventually break them down into their more harmless component parts.

This is not the case with PFOA. Instead, studies have shown that there is no known form of biodegradation to which PFOA is susceptible. Quite simply, it is not affected by the actions of microorganisms, sunlight, or water. In fact, scientists think that it may be the most persistent manmade chemical every created. In the most basic terms, they believe that PFOA literally lasts forever.

This means that PFOA is permanently accumulating in the environment in ever greater quantities as increasing amounts are added to our air, water and soil both during the manufacture of PFC-based materials and then again when these materials break down during use. And that brings us to the second thing scientists have discovered about PFOA and other PFCs: Like many chlorinated compounds, they are also accumulating in our bodies.

Fifteen PFC-related chemicals have been detected in human blood and tissues. That's every single PFC compound for which researches have so far tested people. This contamination is so widespread that it appears to be nearly universal. A study conducted by Scotchgard-maker 3M, for example, checked the blood of 598 children from 23 states and the District of Columbia and found PFOA in 96 percent of the tested samples. The levels in adult bloodstreams throughout the country are similar.[1] Scientists estimate that 90 percent of the American population has some level of PFC contamination.[2]

Current evidence suggests that PFOA has a half-life of 4.4 years in the human body. That is, after 4.4 years, the amount of PFOA in blood and bodily tissues should be reduced by 50 percent. After another 4.4 years, the remaining 50 percent should be reduced by half again for a total reduction of 75 percent, and so on. But this scenario assumes that there are no additional exposures to PFOA, a circumstance that's highly unlikely at best in what is fast becoming a PFOA-saturated world.

Just how much PFOA and other PFCs has been released into the environment? No one really knows. That's because PFCs are completely unregulated. Manufacturers are legally free to release unlimited quantities into our air, water, and soils, and no law what-soever exists to mandate either the monitoring or reporting of these emissions. We do know that approximately 660 tons of PFOA are produced each year in the United States.[3] We also know from industry studies supplied to the EPA that many tons of PFOA have been released from facilities operated by DuPont and 3M (the primary makers of PFCs). For example, DuPont reports releasing 10 tons of PFOA from its Washington Works Teflon production plant in West Virginia in 2002.[4] To these industrial releases of PFOA, we must add all the countless small quantities of PFOA being released into the environ-ment in homes and offices as the PFCs in non-stain and non-stick products break down over time. And we must remember that experts believe that PFOA is likely un-biodegrad-able and will never go away. All the new PFOA introduced into our environment each year is simply added to all of the PFOA that's ever been released.

The ubiquitous presence of PFOA and other PFCs in our products, environment, and bodies is troubling for many reasons. In an as-yet-unreleased report, an EPA Science Advisory Board has declared that the weight of evidence shows PFOA to be a "likely car-cinogen."[5] Indeed, the chemical has been linked to testicular, pancreatic, breast, liver.[6] and bladder cancer.[7] It is also a hormonal disruptor known to cause increased levels of estro-gen and abnormal testosterone regulation in the body. In addition, PFOA can damage the thyroid gland and cause hyperthyroidism, a condition that can affect hearing and brain development. PFOA also disrupts the immune system by damaging a variety of different kinds of immune cells responsible for protecting us from illness. (Scientists, in fact, have yet to identify a PFOA exposure level that does not cause immune system dysfunction; as far as immunotoxicity is concerned, PFOA appears to be hazardous in even the most minute amounts.) And, as if that isn't enough, PFOA is also can cause reproductive and developmental problems like low birth weight, decreased growth, and birth defects.[8]

All this information leaves us with one very important question: What can consumers do to protect themselves from PFOA exposures? The key is to keep further exposures to an absolute minimum by keeping PFC-based products out of the home. That means tak-ing steps like these:

- Avoid non-stick pans and cookware. In addition to releasing PFOA over time, tests show that these items release hazardous fumes when heated during even normal use. Instead, invest in cast iron cookware and take the time to properly season it. (Seasoning is a process by which a cast iron surface is coated with shortening and then baked in order to create a smooth, slick surface.) A well-seasoned pan will func-tion just like one coated in Teflon — foods slide right out and cleanup is a breeze.

- If you choose to use a non-stick pan or other similarly coated cookware, never apply heat to it while it's empty. Empty cookware gets very hot very quickly, and overheating causes the non-stick coating to break down more rapidly and release large amounts of toxins in a single burst. Water, cooking oils, and other liquids absorb heat and can help prevent this process.

- When you purchase carpet or upholstered furniture, shop for products that are not pre-treated for stain resistance and refuse any such additional treatments that stores or manufacturers may offer. Note that while 3M reformulated its famous Scotchgard treatment in 2001 in response to concerns about PFOA, the reformulation relies on a compound called PFBS, which is chemically related to PFOS and may present similar problems. (Because PFBS remains largely unstudied, we urge a precautionary approach.)

- Don't buy or wear clothing that says it's been treated to repel water, dirt, or stains.

- Cut out as much processed food as you can from your diet and avoid fast foods, especially greasy types. Many of the containers used to package these kinds of foods are coated with PFCs in order to prevent grease and oils from soaking through. This especially true where paper- and cardboard-based packaging is concerned. If you choose to buy processed and other "convenience" foods, remove them from their original packaging as soon as possible and store and heat them in glass, metal or ceramic containers instead.

- Do not use microwave popcorn, which is typically sold and prepared in PFC-coated bags. Instead, combine a quarter cup of high quality popping corn in a regular unbleached brown paper lunch bag, mix with the recommended amount of oil and any desired seasoning, fold over the opening, and staple the bag with a single staple. (Don't worry — that's not enough metal to cause sparking!) Heat for two to three minutes or use the popcorn setting on your microwave.

- Be careful what kind of paper plates you use at picnics and other events. If the plate looks glossy, don't use it. As with much fast-food packaging, the plates may be coated with PFCs to prevent leakage.

- Scrutinize personal care, cosmetic, and cleaning product labels carefully. Avoid those with any ingredient that contains "fluoro" or "perfluoro" as part of its name. This indicates the presence of a PFC.

- Be wary of dental floss. Many brands are coated with a type of Teflon called PTFE. Stick to plain, unwaxed varieties.

Beating a Better Path to a Healthier Bath

Depending upon what's being used to clean it, another hub of potential toxicity in the average home is the bathroom. If the cleaning challenges we face in the kitchen seem tough, those found in our bathrooms are downright apocalyptic. These hotbeds of humidity can and often do harbor disproportionate amounts of bacteria, molds, and mildew, not to mention annoyances like soap scum, rust stains, and hard water scale produced by our constant use of water. No wonder that in getting our bathrooms clean and keeping them that way we tend to reach for one of the widest array of cleaners that we carry into any room in the house.

Unfortunately, traditional bathroom cleaners employ some of the more toxic chemical formulas of all of the household products that we regularly buy. These products, after all, are designed largely to either kill living organisms or vaporize seemingly impenetrable deposits of various kinds. For these reasons, they tend to contain biologically active poisons disguised as "disinfectants" and/or strong acids and solvents that literally eat away at anything that's not porcelain, glass, or metal. (And some of them even eat away metal!)

As is the case elsewhere in our homes, when we use these products in the bathroom we're exposing our families to the hazards they contain whether it's via toxic fumes that can be inhaled or hazardous residues that remain behind after the product is used. Label warnings like "Use in well ventilated areas," "Avoid prolonged breathing of vapor," "For sensitive skin wear gloves," and "Not recommended for persons with asthma or heart conditions," give you some insight into the kinds of chemicals these products contain and the hazards they leave behind.

A better strategy is to take preventative action to stop problems before they get started, and to use natural materials and formulas whenever cleaning is needed. Here are some ways to keep the need for serious bathroom cleaning to a minimum:

- Whenever showering or bathing, keep as much fresh air circulating through your bathroom as possible. Ventilating your bathroom via open windows, exhaust fans, or other means will help prevent moisture from building up and feeding mold and mildew growth.

- Fix leaks and drips whenever and wherever you find them. The drier your bathroom is, the cleaner and healthier it will stay.

- Clean up puddles and spills as soon as they happen for the same reason. Never let water sit for any period of time.

- If your shower has a door, leave it open after you bathe.

- If mold and/or mildew is a particular problem, consider wiping down tub and shower surfaces with a squeegee or towel after use.

- Clean mold and/or mildew as soon as any is spotted. Don't let these colonies of microorganisms grow and spread before you take action. It's a lot easier to clean a small initial patch than it is an entire shower stall!

- Close the toilet lid before you flush. Though you can't see it happening, the act of flushing a toilet sends thousands of micro-droplets of toilet bowl water into the air and onto bathroom surfaces. Closing the lid prevents these droplets from escaping and spreading any bacteria they may contain.

- Wash your faucet handles more frequently than other surfaces and/or give a daily quick spritz of hydrogen peroxide or tea tree oil solution (see below). Since they are usually touched by hands before those hands have been washed, faucet handles can be hot spots of bacterial contamination.

- Understand and accept that you'll never be able to completely sanitize your bathroom. It's not only impossible, it might not even be desirable. (See more about why in Chapter 20.) Don't try to keep every surface hyperclean all the time. Unless you have someone at home suffering from an immune disease, it's not necessary.

- Once they're clean, give your bathroom and its surfaces a quick once-over every week to prevent new problems from starting.

When it comes to the cleaners you use in the bathroom, seek those with formulas based on vegetable and other non-toxic sources. As is the case in other categories of cleaning products, a number of manufacturers have ingeniously combined new technologies with time-tested old-fashioned raw materials to create bathroom cleaners that work like their toxic conventional counterparts but without any hazards to your health. These products use safe biodegradable ingredients to clean and sanitize surfaces, banish mildew, polish tubs and sinks, and more.

Your can also make your own bathroom cleaners using just a few basic non-toxic materials. Here's a look at some safe and effective recipes that get the job done:

(Again, we recommend *Better Basics for the Home,* by Annie Berthold Bond, a virtual encyclopedia of formulas and preparations for the healthy home, for more information about these and other cleaning methods.)

- **Toilets** can be cleaned with either vinegar or baking soda, depending on what ails them. Vinegar will work well on mineral build-up. Baking soda will handle common soils. Apply these materials separately for maximum effect. If deodorization is desired, perform a final scrub with some peppermint or another essential oil after your cleaners have been flushed away. For sanitation, either spray with hydrogen peroxide or use a combination of two tablespoons of tea tree oil in two cups of water. Add some of this to the bowl, scrub, let soak for a few minutes, and flush. (Note that hydrogen peroxide is affected by exposure to light. If you choose to keep a preloaded spray bottle around the house, that bottle should block light and be stored in a dark place.)

- **Sinks and countertops** can be scrubbed with baking soda and water. Add a few drops of natural liquid soap like Dr. Bronner's if more than scouring is required. Borax can be substituted for the baking soda if deodorizing is required. For really tough scouring challenges, try a 1:1 combination of baking soda and washing soda. (Note that this combination should not be used on fiberglass because it can scratch that material.) Use gloves when you scrub because washing soda can be caustic. For a fresh scent, add a few drops of essential oil to the method of your choice

- **Showers, tubs, and tile** can be cleaned with these same materials and formulas.

- **Soap scum** can be removed with vinegar. Simply soak the affected area and wash clean. For tough scum problems combine one teaspoon of borax with half a teaspoon of liquid soap and two cups of hot water. Spray and sponge clean.

- **Hard water scale** can be handled by a spray consisting of one quarter of a cup of white distilled vinegar or lemon juice with a half teaspoon of liquid soap and three quarters of a cup of hot water. Spray the affected area, let stand for a few minutes, and rinse. For encrusted shower curtains or liners (either cloth or plastic), simply wash the offending article in a washing machine using hot water, the usual amount of detergent, and a cup of vinegar.

- **Rust stains** will disappear when subjected to a solution consisting of one tablespoon of cream of tartar and enough hydrogen peroxide (the same common three percent solution sold in drug stores) to make a paste. Apply to cover the stain and let sit for several hours.

- **Mold and mildew** can be eradicated with a simple solution of two tablespoons of tea tree oil in two cups of water. Spray on the affected area, let sit for half an hour, and then wipe clean. This formula also kills bacteria. You can also spray the affected area with vinegar followed immediately by a spray with hydrogen peroxide.

Devils in the Dust

From the grandest mansion to the humblest cottage, all homes share one thing in common, and that's dust. No matter how hard we scrub or how cleanly we live, there's no escaping this ever-present scourge of microscopic particles.

Incredibly, some 43 million tons of dust settle over the United States each year. Thirty-one million of these tons are from natural sources and 12 million tons are man-made.[8] The average home's share of all this accumulating dust is about 40 pounds per year.[9]

When shafts of sunlight enter our homes at the right angle we can see some of this dust swirling hypnotically through the air. These visible particles are about 20-30 microns in size. But many particles that make up our home's dust are much smaller. Depending on their origins, dust particles can be as small as 1/100 of a micron or 1/10,000 the width of a human hair.[10] These particles can't be seen with the naked eye and are so small that they're easily able to pass through the filtration systems in the nose, throat, and lungs.

Where much of the dust in our homes are concerned, this isn't a big worry. That's because the bulk of the dust that surrounds us consists of minute particles of natural materials like skin, hair, pollen, mold, fungi, lichen, wood, natural fabric fibers, plant and vegetable matter, insect parts, and paper fibers. Our immune systems have been dealing with these particles for thousands of years and have become quite adept at coping with any threat they might represent.

But there are other less savory things in dust as well. Modern dust is contaminated by a wide variety of modern pollutants. It's not uncommon to find some combination of soot, pesticides, hydrocarbons, synthetic chemicals, flame retardants, paint, heavy metals, and other toxins hiding in the typical sample. Indeed, a 2005 study by Clean Production

Action tested dust from the vacuum cleaner bags in 70 homes across 7 states for 44 different toxins in 6 categories: PBDE flame retardants; phthalates, a common plasticizer and consumer product additive; organotin compounds, another common consumer product additive found in diapers, foams, food packaging and other places; alkylphenols, a class of chemicals found in cleaning products and cosmetics; Perfluorinated organics, compounds created by non-stick cookware and stain-resistant materials and coatings; and pesticides. The study created composite samples from each state and found that at least one chemical from each of the chosen categories was present in each sample tested.[11]

≈ It's not uncommon to find some combination of pesticides, hydrocarbons, chemicals, heavy metals, and other toxins hiding in the typical dust sample. ≈

Another ubiquitous component of dust is dust mites, which live by the billions in the mattresses, furniture, carpeting, and dust of the average home. A single ounce of dust can contain 42,000 of these microscopic creatures. For most of us, this is none too pleasant to think about but hardly a worry. However, an estimated 10 percent of all Americans and as many as 90 percent of all sufferers of allergic asthma are allergic to the proteins found in the wastes dust mites produce and the body parts they leave behind.[12]

It's with these ideas in mind that the act of dusting takes on a new importance. Here are some ways in which you can keep your home as dust-free as possible as safely as possible:

- Be aware that dust in modern homes can be contaminated by toxic flame-retardants called PBDEs, which, in case we haven't provided you with enough chemical tongue twisters already, is thankfully short for polybrominateddiphenylethers. This issue has only recently been discovered. According to those who've studied it, the PBDEs added to household foams, electronic devices, and other products can easily leave those products and settle in household dust. This is because PBDEs don't bond to their host materials on a molecular level. Instead, they're free to migrate out of whatever material they've been added to and wander. For this reason, when you buy a new computer, make sure it's PBDE-free. Apple, Toshiba, Dell, NEC, and Hewlett Packard are among the companies now offering equipment made without PBDEs. If you're unsure about whether or not a particular piece of gear is safe, call the manufacturer before you buy it. Employ a similar strategy for any electronic device.

- Don't open the case of your computer for cleaning or upgrades. Instead, take your machine to an outside location for professional servicing. Internal computer components become extremely dusty over time and this dust is easily and often contaminated with PBDEs that are then released into the air when disturbed by cleaning or maintenance.

- Clean the outside of your computer with a vacuum that has a HEPA filter. These filters catch dust and trap it for safe removal away from the home. Many vacuums blow the smaller particles they catch back out into the air. HEPA filtration prevents this recirculation and isolates all PBDE-contaminated dust you capture.

- Use the same HEPA vacuum on floors and surfaces. Vacuum floors and upholstered surfaces at least once a week to avoid dust build-up. Vacuum or wash curtains or drapes frequently. If you have dust mite allergies, add mattresses to the vacuuming list.

- Steam-clean carpets and upholstery at least once a year to get a deep-down fresh start.

- Over time (and we're sorry to have to say it!), a pillow can have up to half its weight taken up by dust mites and associated particles. For this reason, experts recommend occasionally washing your pillows in the washing machine. Wash feather pillows two at a time using the delicate cycle and just a small amount of detergent. Give the pillows an extra rinse when the cycle completes, and dry them in a dryer set on low with several clean sneakers to help fluff them back up.

- Wash bedding and mattress pads once a week in hot water to kill any dust mites that are present. If you or a family member are especially allergic to dust or dust mites, use protective covers for your pillows and mattresses. (Look for special anti-allergy covers sold for this purpose.)

- When dusting, don't use a feather duster or other similar tool. These simply stir settled dust back into the air where it can be more easily inhaled. Instead, use a damp cloth and rinse it frequently in a bucket. This will help you actually remove accumulated dust from the home rather than simply redistribute it. Statically-charged dusters that actually attract and hold dust rather that simply scatter it around can also be used.

- Replace furniture and car seats that have torn upholstery and exposed foam to prevent their PBDEs from entering your home.

- Similarly, exercise caution when removing or replacing foam padding beneath carpets. Take care to disturb the dust collected there as little as possible. Quickly isolate the old padding and remove it from the home.

- Before buying new furniture, make sure the manufacturer isn't using PBDEs. Ikea is one chain that has removed these chemicals from its products. When possible, avoid furniture that contains foam. Opt instead for a natural fiber stuffing like cotton and wool.

• Consider replacing carpeting with wood or other hard flooring accented by washable area rugs. Unlike carpets, hard floors don't trap dust, pollutants, or allergens and can be easily and frequently swept clean.

• If your home is particularly dusty, or if you are particularly sensitive, wear a dust mask when cleaning to avoid inhaling any dust you disturb.

• Don't use traditional commercial spray cleaners or furniture waxes when dusting (or at any other time for that matter). These contain a wide variety of synthetic chemicals and pound for pound represent some of the most toxic cleaning products available.

• Track your home's humidity with a humidity monitor. Dust mites prefer humidity levels over 50 percent. If your air contains too much moisture, use a dehumidifier.

• Keep all your home's walkways and entrances free of dirt, soils, and other things that can get tracked into the house and converted to dust.

• Make liberal use of welcome mats around doors to remove particles attached to shoes before those shoes enter your home. Clean and vacuum these mats regularly to make sure they don't become a source of dust themselves.

• Consider asking guests and family members to remove their shoes whenever they enter your home, especially in urban areas. Shoes are one of the prime conduits by which pollutants enter the typical house.

• Cut down on your clutter. Clutter not only attracts dust, it makes it harder to clean effectively. Whenever and wherever you can, store and display collections and knick knacks in glass cabinets or display cases.

• Do not allow smoking in your home. Tobacco smoke contributes to the particulate pollution burden your home's dust carries.

30

Fighting the Fungus Among Us

In recent years there have been a number of widely publicized reports in the popular press about mold running amok in the homes of unsuspecting citizens. Like some 1950s B-grade horror movie, tales of killer fungus taking over entire houses and forcing the relocation of their now deathly ill occupants have brought the issue of household mold into the forefront of the home front.

In truth, some molds can present very serious health problems. Fortunately, infestations of these species are relatively uncommon. Yet even small amounts of common and generally harmless molds can release microscopic spores that trigger allergic reactions or other health problems.

To help prevent mold from gaining a foothold in your home:

- Maintain an indoor relative humidity of 50 percent or lower. Molds need moisture, so deprive them of it. Get a humidity gauge and use dehumidifiers in chronically damp areas.

- Don't over-water your houseplants. Keep the soil moist but not soaked.

- Make sure your clothes dryer is vented to the outside.

- Fix leaks in your plumbing quickly. Even a minor leak that looks harmless can be soaking your home inside its walls and creating soggy conditions that you can't see.

- Whenever water damage occurs in your home or items like carpets get wet, they should be dried within two days to prevent mold growth from starting. Replace any materials that are too wet to dry in that amount of time.

- When showering or bathing, open windows and/or use exhaust vents that carry humid air outside. Adopt the same strategy in the kitchen when dishwashers are running or cooking is taking place for an extended period.
- If local mold counts are high, keep your windows and doors closed.

To clean mold and mildew see our recipe for a natural mold-killing cleaner on page 96.

31

Clearly Cleaner Windows

Everyone hates to clean windows. The work is hard, and there's a lot of it. But the consequences of ignoring this chore are even worse. Dirty windows lower the levels of natural light that's able to enter our homes, limit our views outside, and can make even the cleanest room seem dingy. For these and other reasons, to each window a proper cleaning must eventually come. When it does, we tend to reach for commercial glass cleaners that make the easiest go of one of housekeeping's toughest tasks.

It's no surprise to learn that most commercial glass cleaners are a blend of synthetic chemicals, many of which are toxic. Though regulatory loopholes and a lack of labeling laws prevent us from knowing exactly what particular hazards are found in which specific products, we can make some educated generalizations about the kinds of ingredients traditional glass cleaners are likely to contain. These chemicals include:

- **Solvents to loosen and dissolve dirt, and speed product evaporation.** Solvents typically found in glass cleaners include butyl cellosolve, naphtha, and glycol ethers, all toxins that are easily absorbed by the skin and capable of doing neurological, respiratory, and organ damage. Such solvents are also commonly contaminated by benzene, a known carcinogen.

- **Petroleum waxes that "dirt-proof" glass.** Many consumer glass cleaners contain synthetic waxes that remain behind after the product has evaporated. These waxes coat glass with a soil-resistant surface that builds up as the cleaner is used over time and eventually forms a seemingly impenetrable seal.

- **Phosphoric acid or ammonia to cut through grime and dirt.** These two highly corrosive irritants act like a chemical booster shot that assists the product's solvents in removing a surface's more stubborn soils faster and with less scrubbing.

- **Synthetic dyes and perfumes.** The majority of these ingredients are derived from suspect sources, primarily petroleum and toxic coal tars. When it comes to health effects, artificial colorants and scents remain largely untested. Because they are added to product formulas for purely aesthetic reasons, there's no need to risk exposure to any potential hazards they represent.

Compounding the issue of toxic ingredients in glass cleaners is the fact that these products are applied via spraying. Spraying disperses these poisons over a wide area beyond the window itself and produces aerosols, incredibly fine particles of mist that can remain suspended in the air for extended periods of time and travel over relatively long distances in the home. The creation of aerosols means that you and your family will still be inhaling minute quantities of glass cleaner long after the cleaning is finished and possibly even in rooms where no cleaning occurred.

As is the case with our other cleaning dilemmas, the answer is to use natural materials to clean the windows and glass in your home. Unfortunately, there's probably no household challenge that's done more to damage the reputation of natural cleaners and homemade cleaning products than dirty windows. That's because the alternative most of us have heard about is vinegar wiped off with old newspaper, a method that can't effectively remove the synthetic waxes left behind by traditional glass cleaners. The result of this uneven match-up is streaky windows that look even worse than they did before and countless well-intentioned homeowners who are now convinced that natural solutions are inferior.

Nothing, of course, could be further from the truth. Here's how to get your windows, mirrors, computer and TV screens, and other glass surfaces safely clean and kept that way:

- If you want to buy a safe window cleaner, consult the chart on page 168 for those that pass our non-toxic test. Keep in mind that because of the waxes in traditional cleaners you may have to clean the window several times to get the sparkle you're looking for.

- If you want to make your own window cleaner, invest in a good quality window squeegee and a spray bottle. Fill the spray bottle with a mixture of two cups of water and one quarter cup of distilled vinegar.

- The first time or two you clean your windows, add a half teaspoon or so of natural liquid soap to your homemade window cleaner. Use more or less soap depending on whether your concentration isn't cutting through the wax or is sudsing too much and requires rinsing.

- Apply the spray, scrub the window with the squeegee scrubber, and squeegee the liquid over and down to a single corner, which you can wipe with a rag or a recycled paper towel. (We don't like using newspapers because their synthetic ink gets everywhere and using them for windows means they can't be recycled.)

- Use a lint-free chamois cloth to polish streaks away.

- If your windows aren't too dirty, or have only a small area that needs to be cleaned (like a computer monitor), new "microfiber" cleaning cloths will do an excellent job without any cleaning formula of any kind.

32

What to Pour on Your Floor

Modern homes are often filled with a bewildering variety of flooring. Indeed, in terms of the creativity now being applied in the world of interior design, the sky would seem to be the limit as traditional standbys like carpet, wood, linoleum, vinyl, and tile meet new materials like stone, bamboo, cement, cork, and even recycled automobile tires.

While the ever-growing number of flooring options does give us more to choose from, it often results in consternation when it comes to cleaning. Can we wash our kitchen's tile floor with the same product we use to clean our wood-floored foyer? Will our bamboo bathroom buckle if we bring in a bucket of vinyl cleaner? Just what should we use, and where should we use it?

All too often the answer is that no one really knows for sure, and manufacturers only add to our confusion by providing a nearly endless supply of different products and formulas tailored to this use or that.

Like other categories of household cleaning products, floor cleaners, polishes, and waxes are mixtures of many different chemicals. In addition to synthetic detergents, fragrances, and dispersal and suspension agents, such products often include hazardous organic solvents to help dissolve tough soils and speed drying times.

Products meant to shine and polish floors are deliberately designed to leave residues behind. These cleaners usually contain synthetic waxes and polymers, which remain on floors to provide a sheen after the liquid has evaporated. Typically, such products also contain strong acids or solvents, which dissolve the previous wash's coating so that dirt can be lifted from it.

What manufacturers don't want you to know is that you can clean most of the floors in your home with just two things: old-fashioned soap and nice hot water. While owners of specialty flooring should always check to be sure their particular type is a candidate for such easy care, for the most part soap and water are all you need to make floors shine.

- You can also make a safe and effective floor cleaner by combining one quarter cup of natural liquid soap with half a cup of distilled vinegar and two gallons of hot water. Add a few drops of your favorite essential oil to this formula for a fresh scent if desired.

≈ For the most part soap and water are all you need to make floors shine. ≈

- For wood floors, substitute a teaspoon of glycerin for the vinegar in the above formula.

- For tough soils or greasy problem areas replace the vinegar in the above formula with one quarter cup of washing soda. Note that washing soda will remove wax. This is ideal if you want to remove synthetic wax from your floor for a truly clean start. But if you want the wax to stay, keep the washing soda away.

- Polish wood floors with jojoba or boiled linseed oil. Just apply the oil, wipe, and polish. But be careful: this can make your floor very slippery!

- For carpet cleaning, rent a steam cleaner from a local hardware store and fill it with a formula of one eighth of a cup of liquid soap and two gallons of hot water. Add a half teaspoon of borax or washing soda per quart of water to increase the cleaning power on dirtier carpets.

- Forget using a sponge mop and invest in a good string mop and a wringer bucket. These clean your floor faster and more efficiently.

33

Airing Our Dirty Laundry

Got laundry? Who doesn't! In homes all across the land, it's the chore that's never finished. While you were doing that final load of what you were sure was absolutely every last shirt and stray sock in the house, a new pile was sprouting somewhere on somebody's bedroom floor. It's enough to send your head into a permanent spin cycle. Yet though we practically live in our laundry rooms, we're often unaware of what's really going on in there and just what all these dirty duds are doing to the world.

According to Project Laundry List, about 35 billion loads of laundry are washed each year in the US. That's 100 million pounds of pants and petticoats. The average household washes about 50 pounds of laundry in 7.4 weekly loads, each of which contains roughly 16 items. In a typical household over 6,000 items are laundered in a year. Every second of every day approximately 1,000 loads of laundry are started. Of these, 50 percent are warm water loads, 35 percent cold, and 15 percent hot. And 90 percent are dried in a clothes dryer.[1]

That's a lot of laundry, and it creates a big environmental impact. Washing and drying the fabrics of our lives is water-intensive, energy-intensive, and responsible for the release of toxic chemicals and other unhealthy synthetics into local soils and waters. It consumes resources and creates pollution, and to add insult to injury, it isn't even fun! So what can we do to keep both our clothes and environment clean? Try these ideas on for size:

- Use laundry detergents made from natural, readily biodegradable ingredients. Synthetic detergents contain surfactants made from petrochemicals. These pollute water outside the home and leave residues on clothes. Non-toxic laundry products use readily biodegradable ingredients made from natural materials like vegetable oils instead.

- Check detergent labels and avoid gimmicks like optical brighteners that coat clothes with a chemical that reflects light to trick the eye and make whites appear whiter.

- Use alternatives to chlorine bleach (a.k.a. sodium hypochlorite). Chlorine bleach can harm certain fabrics. It can combine with the organic matter present in the dirt in our clothes to form chlorinated hydrocarbons that include carcinogens like dioxins, chlorinated furans, and trihalomethanes, and hundreds of other toxins. These toxins are also created when chlorine bleach is released into the environment via wastewater and combines with natural organic materials present in soils and water. Instead of chlorine bleach, use hydrogen peroxide-based bleaches, also known as oxygen bleaches. These are far gentler on fabrics and break down into water and oxygen in the environment. Sodium percarbonate, which is made by combining hydrogen peroxide with the mineral sodium carbonate, is a similarly benign alternative.

- Use the cold water wash option whenever possible and you'll save 85 percent of the money and energy consumed by a hot water load, and help prevent climate change. (The energy used to heat your water supply is one of your home's largest contributors to global warming.) Wash full loads to get the most out of whatever water, energy, and detergent you do use.

- Electric dryers cost over $75 dollars a year to operate. Gas dryers fare little better. So air dry your clothes on a line. The sun's energy is non-polluting and free for the taking. In winter, string a line in the basement or laundry room and use the heat that's already circulating in your home to get the job done.

- When shopping for a new washing machine and/or clothes dryer look for the Department of Energy (DOE) Energy Star seal of approval. This designation indicates machines that use less power and/or water.

- Consider a front-loading washing machine. These are kinder to clothes and use up to 36 percent less water and 60 percent less energy.

- Be aware that new DOE regulations mandating increased washing machine efficiency are scheduled to take effect in 2007. If you can wait another year to replace your washer, the payoff will be huge as this new generation of washers will use 35 percent less energy and water in every load.

34

Ten Safety Precautions for Using Chemical Cleaners

We believe that synthetic chemical-based household cleaners are sufficiently dangerous to preclude their use in the home. Given the many serious health and environmental hazards associated with the ingredients they contain, we don't recommend them in any way for any purpose. However, we also realize that many consumers may prefer them for certain tasks. For those who make the choice to continue to use toxic chemical cleaners, we've created this list of safety precautions. They can help lower your exposure risk to the hazardous ingredients found in many cleaners. Please keep in mind, however, that no amount of precautionary action can completely prevent the dangers related to the use of such products.

1. **Protect your children.** Do not use chemical cleaners when children are present. Even minute quantities can affect them. The organization Boston Physicians for Social Responsibility believes, for example, that there is absolutely no safe level of exposure for neurotoxins, chemicals that many cleaning products contain. If chemical cleaners must be used, apply them when children are at school or away from home. Do not under any circumstances ever use any chemical cleaner in a child's bedroom. Either use natural cleaners, plain water, or don't clean at all! Using chemical cleaning products in a child's bedroom will expose them to far higher levels of toxins because of the disproportionate amount of time children spend in their rooms playing and sleeping.

2. **Ventilate.** Keep fresh air coming into your house while you use chemical cleaners. Open windows and doors (even in winter!), use fans, and run air conditioners. This air exchange will remove some of the pollutants to the outside and reduce the concentrations of any airborne contaminants that remain.

3. **Wear protective clothing.** This includes heavy-duty gloves, a breathing mask, long-sleeved clothing, full-length pants, and safety goggles. If you feel like you're dressing up for hazardous waste duty, you're right! As we've seen, the very products you're using are considered just that when you place them in your trash can. Strong physical protection measures definitely apply. Cleaning product chemicals can enter the body via your skin, lungs, stomach, and mucous membranes, and in most cases users are unaware this entry is occurring. Protecting your bodily surfaces from exposure safeguards you to a limited extent.

4. **Buy only small quantities of toxic cleaners.** Purchasing only what you need will prevent the accumulation of old leftover products that must then be disposed of as hazardous waste or, worse, might simply remain in your home for years.

5. **Don't use hot water.** Hot water allows the volatile chemicals found in many cleaners to evaporate more easily and enter the air in greater amounts. Using warm or cool water will help keep the chemicals you're using more contained and keep the air you're breathing healthier.

6. **Never mix cleaners.** You may accidentally create substances more hazardous than any of the individual cleaners alone.

7. **Rinse thoroughly.** Rinsing cleaned surfaces thoroughly and repeatedly will remove as much cleaning product residue as possible. And the more you can remove, the healthier your home will be.

8. **Avoid waxes and polishes.** Products intended to make surfaces shiny are specifically designed to leave residues behind and usually contain dangerous solvents that help keep the active ingredients in suspension in the product and make it dry faster. **Similarly, avoid toilet bowl and oven cleaners.** These products typically contain harsh acids or caustics, chlorinated chemicals and bleaches, and/or large amounts of solvents, which combine to give these categories of products what is generally the highest toxic load of any kind of cleaner.

9. **Don't use spray cleaners.** Spray cleaners diffuse their chemicals directly into the air over a wide area and distribute these substances across distances that often exceed those areas being cleaned. Cleaners you mix in a bucket and/or apply directly by hand via a sponge or rag stay more self-contained and are easier to control.

10. **Exercise extra caution in the kitchen.** As is the case with children's rooms, make an exception and keep synthetic cleaners away from eating, food prep, and cooking areas. If you're hesitant to try natural cleaners, these areas are ideal places to experiment and see how easy such products can be to use.

Kidstuff

THE SUBJECT OF CONVENTIONAL HOUSEHOLD CHEMICALS looms largest where the smallest members of our families are concerned. Simply put, children are most susceptible to the dangers presented by the chemicals in consumer products. Compared to adults, they have a far greater chance of developing health problems as a result of exposure to the toxins hiding in everything from cleaning products to toys.

If we're vigilant when it comes to our own health, we need to be hyperprotective when it comes to safeguarding our kids. That means understanding just how sensitive they are to synthetic chemicals and knowing how to keep the greatest risks away.

35

Why Our Littlest Ones Face the Largest Risk From Our Homes' Biggest Hazards

Though our kids may not seem to be generally any more or less at risk than ourselves from exposure to household cleaners and other chemical products, nothing could be further from the truth. In fact, children are much more likely than grown-ups to develop both short- and long-term health problems as a result of contact with common consumer chemicals. For example, the National Academy of Sciences has estimated that 25 percent of developmental and neurological deficits in children can be traced to the interaction between synthetic chemicals and genetic factors, and that 3 percent are triggered by chemicals alone.[1] The reasons for these dramatically increased odds are fairly simple.[2]

1. **Children wrap big appetites in a small package and experience greater exposures to the toxins in household cleaners on a bodyweight basis as a result.** Pound for pound, kids drink more water and eat more food than the average adult. For example, babies in the first half year of life drink seven times more water per pound of body weight than the typical grown-up. Children between the ages of one and five consume three to four times more food per pound of body weight than the average adult. They also inhale more air than adults. The amount of air inhaled by a resting infant per pound of bodyweight, for example, is twice that of his or her parents. Whenever a home's water, food, or air is contaminated by chemicals, the children living there will experience significantly greater exposures to these toxins than will the adults in their family.

2. **Children live and play where much of the toxicological action is, and their instinctive behavior magnifies this risk.** The younger they are, the closer to the

ground kids live, and ground level is where many of the household pollutants introduced by cleaning products tend to settle. Floors tend to act as "toxic sinks" that concentrate chemical poisons. They collect vapors that are heavier-than-air, contaminated dust that falls to the ground, and traces of cleaners that have been applied to floors or simply end up there after being used elsewhere in the home. In addition, young children naturally put everything in their mouths. From dirty hands to that strange piece of goodness-knows-what they found under the chair, kids explore their world largely through hand-to-mouth contact. When those hands are playing in contaminated areas, any contamination they've encountered ends up being eaten.

3. **Children are still growing.** Their bodies are much different than those of adults because they are constantly changing and developing at an often rapid pace. New tissues are being formed, organs are growing, and the nervous system is expanding. The lungs, for example, don't finish developing until about age 20.[3] This growth can be easily disrupted by exposure to common cleaning chemicals. Equal amounts of the same chemical may produce a much different effect in a child than in an adult because the adult's body isn't developing like the body of the growing child. For example, a cleaning solvent capable of interfering with the formation of nerve cells would do much more damage in a child, whose brain is still working to create those cells, than in an adult, whose brain and body built all its nerve cells long ago. Kids' detoxification and immune systems also remain works-in-progress until about age ten.[4] As a result, their bodies are neither able to process and remove toxins nor defend against them as effectively as an adult's.

≈ Childhood illnesses linked to chemical contamination of the environment cost Americans approximately $55 billion dollars each year. ≈

4. **Children have more of their life ahead of them than adults.** Kids simply have more time than adults to acquire illness or disease as a result of exposure to household cleaning chemicals, and time is often exactly what chemical-related ailments need to develop.[5] In fact, many of the ailments associated with household chemicals take decades to emerge. Whether it's cancer or hormonal disruption, asthma or mental dysfunction, children have a much longer future ahead of them for these and other problems to take root.

These factors mean that our children require a significantly greater degree of protection from modern cleaning products and other common household chemicals than we grown-ups. The costs of failing to provide this extra measure of safety are great indeed. In fact, according to a study by the Mount Sinai School of Medicine, childhood illnesses linked to chemical contamination of the environment cost Americans approximately $55 billion dollars each year. That's nearly three percent of total national health care costs and more than we spend on military research, veterans' benefits, or stroke treatments.[6]

Trouble triggered by exposure to household chemicals can occur before birth, as well. A recent study conducted at England's University of Bristol found that infants exposed to cleaning products while still in the womb were more likely to suffer persistent wheezing during childhood, a key sign of likely asthma development. Researchers studied 14,000 children from birth to age three and a half and found that children born into the top ten percent of families using the most cleaning products during pregnancy were more than twice as likely to suffer from wheezing as children born into those families who had used the fewest. This connection remained even after scientists had taken factors like parental smoking, mold, and family medical histories into account.[7]

36

A Baker's Dozen Ways to Help Kids Breathe Easier

With smaller bodies, higher metabolisms, undeveloped defense systems, and an active lifestyle that puts them closer to life's contaminants, children start out with the odds stacked against them when it comes to staying safe and healthy. This is especially true where sensitive young lungs are concerned. Fortunately, there are simple steps we can take that go a long way toward keeping bad household air and the toxins it contains away from our kids.

1. Use untreated natural bedding. Permanent press and other treated sheets contain formaldehyde that's emitted and inhaled while kids sleep. Similarly, don't buy flame-resistant pajamas or other textiles.

2. Wash bedding at least once a week and keep bedroom humidity below 50 percent. Both steps help reduce or eliminate dust mite allergens.

3. If you use candles, use only non-petroleum candles with cloth wicks and natural essential oil scents. Synthetically scented paraffin and other synthetic wax candles emit unhealthy fumes and soot when burned. Make sure any wick you light does not contain a thin metal strand to help it stand upright. Such wicks emit zinc and tin when burned.

4. Use only natural cosmetic and personal care products, and avoid synthetic scents and perfumes. When your children hug and hang out with you, make sure all they pick up is affection and attention!

5. Keep particleboard and other pressed composite wood products out of your home. These building materials are made with glues and other chemicals that give off dangerous

fumes as they age, including toxic formaldehyde. Buy solid wood furnishings and construction supplies to keep this key component of unhealthy indoor air away. If cost is a factor, use plywood, which doesn't outgas as much, instead of particleboard or fiberboard.

6. Let fresh air into your home frequently even in winter. A good healthy air exchange is worth more than any warmed or cooled air you'll replace and is the best way to rinse out any unhealthy pollutants that have accumulated. Let kids sleep with a window opened as much as possible.

7. At school, request that bus drivers turn off their engines while they wait for classes to get out. Buses emit a wide variety of unhealthy particulates and other air pollutants, amounts of which quickly rise to dangerous levels whenever they idle in one place. Also inquire about your school's pesticide policy. Many schools apply these poisons with no prior notification. Insist that you be told when and where, and what your local school is using.

8. Avoid indoor pools treated with chlorine. Choose those pools that use ozonation, UV light, or biguanide, which is a non-toxic chemical alternative most commonly marketed under the name Baquacil.

9. If you get new carpeting that isn't made of natural materials, air it out thoroughly before installation. Carpeting can contain a wide variety of chemical compounds that outgas. Leaving it unrolled or at least loosely rolled in the garage for a week or two before installation will reduce these levels of emitted hazardous gases. Similarly, refuse any carpet treated with stain repellents, mildew treatments, or other chemicals. Don't install carpets with adhesives. And once they're installed, keep fresh air circulating through the room for a few months.

10. Use only safe non-toxic cleaning products. The hazardous fumes and airborne aerosols created by synthetic chemical cleaners are one of the biggest sources of dangerous air pollution inside the average home.

11. Have furnaces, water heaters, and any other combustion devices in your home inspected and serviced annually to make sure emissions aren't escaping into your living spaces. Vent gas ranges to the outside. And never use kerosene or other portable combustion-type heaters.

12. Use only safe and natural arts and crafts supplies. Avoid products that give off fumes, like many permanent ink markers, rubber cement, paints, etc. Use only those products you've verified are safe.

13. Don't use pesticides or any chemical flea and tick preparations for pets, including flea collars, shampoos, and treatments. Researchers have documented clear links between pesticide products and childhood leukemia.[1]

37

Just Say No to VOCs

Although we've discussed them in previous pages, volatile organic compounds (VOCs) deserve a special mention when it comes to children. Scientists studying the effects of VOC exposure on children both before and after birth have begun to discover that these compounds can produce some startlingly unhealthy effects.

Scientists at the University of Bristol in England, for example, have found that the VOCs contained in air fresheners and aerosol products harm the health of mothers and their babies during both pregnancy and early childhood when those products are used around the house. Researchers tracked the health of some 14,000 children before and after birth and discovered that babies living in those homes where air freshener sticks and sprays were used daily rather than weekly experienced 32 percent more diarrhea and were more likely to suffer earaches. Daily use of aerosol polishes, deodorants, and hairsprays, key sources of consumer product VOCs, was associated with a similar 30 percent increase in cases of diarrhea. Mothers who used these air freshening and aerosol products daily had 10 percent more headaches and were 26 percent more likely to suffer from some form of depression.[1]

An investigation of childhood asthma at Princess Margaret Hospital in Perth, Australia, found that exposure to VOCs in the home is also linked to a higher incidence of asthma. Researchers compared 88 children between 6 months and 3 years of age who had been admitted to the hospital's emergency room and diagnosed with asthma. After measuring the actual levels of VOCs in each household's air, they found that those children with asthma were exposed to significantly higher amounts of VOCs than those without. The VOCs most likely to cause asthma were the common chemicals benzene, ethyl benzene, and toluene. For every ten microgram increase per cubic meter in toluene and benzene concentrations, the risk of asthma jumped by nearly two and three times respectively. The researchers concluded that household exposure to VOCs even at levels below current safety thresholds likely increases the risk of childhood asthma.[2]

As a general rule, VOCs are among the more toxic components of a typical cleaning product formula. In addition to being severe eye, skin, and mucous membrane irritants, the majority are dangerous neurotoxins. These chemicals can also damage the liver, the blood, the lungs, and the kidneys. Most solvent exposures occur when their volatile vapors are inhaled, and even very short contact times can lead to negative health effects.

Unfortunately, solvents remain largely hidden in product formulas and their presence often cannot be directly confirmed by reading labels. However, there are still strategies you can employ to protect your kids from them. The following types of products typically contain solvents and should generally be replaced with non-toxic alternatives:

- Oven cleaners
- Paint removers and strippers
- Degreasers
- All-purpose cleaners
- Furniture, floor, and metal polishes
- Glass cleaners
- Spot removers
- Air fresheners and odor removers

In addition to knowing what general kinds of products may contain solvents, there are often clues on product labels that can tip you off to the presence of VOCs inside. When shopping, scrutinize labels carefully and look for these tell-tale signs:

- Information on the label that says the product is either "combustible" or "flammable." VOCs typically account for the vast majority of the flammability hazards represented by consumer chemical products.

- Precautionary statements on the label warning that the product can cause respiratory irritation and should be avoided by people with asthma, respiratory illnesses, emphysema, etc.

- Recommendations that the product only be used with adequate ventilation or in a well ventilated area and/or

- Recommendations that users avoid breathing product vapors.

- A warning statement that says the product should not be stored in temperatures above 120° F.

- A warning statement that says the product should not be used around flame or open fires.

In those cases where products do list their ingredients, you may find a specific listing of one or more of these common solvents:

- 2-butoxyethanol
- acetone
- alcohols (methanol, isopropyl, etc.)
- benzene or benzol
- butoxy ethanol
- butyl cellosolve
- ethylene glycol
- glycol ethers
- kerosene
- naphthas
- n-Hexane
- methylene chloride
- petroleum distillates
- propylene glycol
- toluene or toluol
- trichloroethylene
- xylene or xylol

For more information about VOCs, see 57.

Phthalates Are No Phun

While common sense dictates that we do everything we can to eliminate our children's exposure to more well-known chemical toxins like solvents, pesticides, and chlorinated chemicals, a number of emerging threats remain largely hidden from most parents.

Key among these is a group of compounds collectively known as phthalates ("fuh-thow-lates"). Many researchers are beginning to think that exposure to phthalates is at least partially responsible for a variety of serious childhood ailments.

Phthalates are a group of industrial compounds widely used in a variety of common products. About 7.6 billion pounds are produced throughout the world each year. The largest use of these chemicals is as a plasticizer in polyvinyl chloride (PVC) and other soft plastic products, including many children's toys. These materials and products rely on phthalates to keep them flexible. Without the addition of phthalate plasticizers, these otherwise pliant materials would be fairly stiff and difficult to use for their intended purposes.

Phthalates are also used as solvents that help keep other ingredients in a chemical formula dissolved and dispersed throughout the product. Their oily texture helps lubricate other materials in a product, and this ability to keep a chemical product evenly mixed makes phthalates an ideal additive in things like cosmetics, personal care products, perfumes, inks, and insect repellents among many others. Phthalates are also used in things like lotions to help them penetrate and soften skin. In fact, these chemicals are now used in so many products and in so many places that they've even begun to appear as contaminants in products that don't purposefully contain them.

Unfortunately, phthalates are easily volatized. This means that they are readily able to leave the product they're used in without any help. Of course, you won't find bits of phthalates falling off your vinyl siding or oozing out of your hairspray. Instead, phthalates usually leave the products they're hiding in as vapors that then enter the human body via the lungs. The "new car smell" we're all so used to, for example, is largely the result of phthalate vapors from vinyl dashboards and other parts evaporating into the air and forming an oily film on the inside of your windshield.

When phthalates enter the body, they can cause all kinds of havoc. New evidence has linked exposure to phthalates to reproductive and developmental disorders, cancer, organ damage, and childhood asthma and allergies. A large study of Swedish children, for example, has found that house dust contaminated by phthalate plasticizers is associated with higher rates of asthma and allergic diseases like eczema, a skin reaction characterized by inflammation and scales.[1]

Researchers examined 400 children between 3 to 8 years of age living in 390 buildings and screened blood samples for common allergens while technicians examined homes and took dust samples. About half of the children in the study had asthma or other persistent allergy symptoms.

Unfortunately, consumers aren't likely to ever see phthalates directly listed as an ingredient on product labels. Instead, these chemicals hide in the products that contain them as unlisted components of primary ingredients like perfumes and so-called inerts. Nonetheless, there are steps we can take to keep these toxins out of our homes and away from our kids.

- Don't buy any product that contains n-butyl benzyl phthalate (BBzP) or di-2-ethylhexyl phthalate (DEHP), two common phthalates associated with childhood health problems. Similarly, avoid products that contain phthalic acid, phthalic anhydride, phthalic glycols, or any ingredient that starts with or contains the nearly unpronounceable letter combination "phth."

- Be very wary of soft flexible plastic and vinyl products. Everything from shower curtains to children's toys, including teething rings and other similar products, can contain phthalates. Before buying a soft plastic item, especially a toy, call the manufacturer and ask them to verify that the product is phthalate-free.

- Use only 100 percent natural cosmetics and personal care products. Synthetic versions of these products are two of the leading sources of phthalates in the home. (But remember that the world "natural" on product labels is unregulated and can mean anything.) Synthetic hair sprays, gels and mousses, antiperspirants and deodorants, nail polishes, and perfumes in particular should be avoided as they can expose your child to phthalates with every hug.

- If you have vinyl flooring, consider replacing it with something else as soon as possible in order to protect children from the phthalates vinyl contains. If replacement isn't an option in the near term, keep children off these surfaces or place carpets or area rugs over them. When installing new flooring choose a non-vinyl option.

- Avoid polymer clays, a key source of childhood exposure to phthalates. According to research conducted by the Vermont Public Interest Research Group common bakeable polymer clays sold under brand names like Sculpey, Fimo, and Cernit contain up to 14 percent phthalates by weight. These phthalates enter children's bodies via hand to mouth contact and by the inhalation of the fumes produced when the clays are baked to create permanent sculptures. A child playing for five minutes with just three and a half ounces of the tested clays, for example, would be exposed to levels of phthalates that exceed the maximum daily exposure standards set for drinking water in Florida and Minnesota. Unfortunately, washing hands isn't much help. Even after adult researchers scrubbed their hands, phthalate residues remained on their skin in measurable amounts.

Instead of phthalate-laden plastic clays, try this simple recipe for a safe and natural clay substitute. It can be made in minutes, will last for weeks, and can even be baked into a semi-permanent state.

A-OK Play Clay

1 cup of flour	1 cup of water
1/4 cup of salt	1 tablespoon of vegetable oil
2 tablespoons of cream of tartar	Food coloring (if desired)

Combine all ingredients in a pot over medium heat and stir. Add food coloring until the desired color intensity is reached. (For a 100 percent pure product, natural dyes like beet and berry juice, etc., can be used instead.) Continue stirring until the clay forms a ball and reaches the consistency of commercial play doughs. Place on foil or wax paper until cool. Store in plastic bag or tightly sealed container.

Tin Soldiers On
An Age-Old Material is a New Toxic Threat

Another newly emergent class of modern toxins is the *organotins,* a family of materials made by chemically combining the metal tin with carbon compounds.

Organotins are found in a wide variety of common household products. Chemists use them in polyurethane, polyester, and silicones to trigger or enhance the chemical reactions that create these materials, and to make the finished product stronger. Organotins are also used in the creation of polyvinyl chloride, or PVC, where they are added to prevent the PVC's polymers from decomposing under the high temperatures needed to process this substance into different products. And they're added to plastics like polyethylene and polypropylene for stability.

Organotin compounds like tributyltin and dimethyltin have become increasingly prevalent in consumer goods over the years. Today, they are found in all kinds of consumer products, including vinyl siding, window frames, and pipe fittings; PVC toys and other products; clear food and beverage containers; food wraps; blister packs like those used for medicines; home furnishings like flooring and wall coverings; fabrics; disposable diapers; and (you guessed it) cleaning products and air fresheners.

This is a trend of no small concern because scientists have found that organotins migrate out of materials that contain them and enter both the environment and people, where they are suspected of bioaccumulating (see page 31). Once inside our bodies, they're capable of disrupting hormonal functions and damaging the immune system by attacking white blood cells.

Because organotins are only now emerging as an environmental health issue, little research into the severity of the problem has yet been conducted. No one currently knows exactly how much organotin exposure we're receiving on a daily basis, how toxic these exposures might be, and whether or not either the exposures or their health effects are cumulative. There are only suspicions that the news might not be good. Until further evidence is gathered, a precautionary approach is advisable. To that end, consumers should:

- Cover any vinyl floors frequented by children with carpets or area rugs.

- Avoid soft plastic toys unless it can be ascertained that they are PVC- and organotin-free.

- Choose tributyltin-free disposable diapers.

- Avoid plastic food wraps, especially those made with PVC (call the manufacturer to find out what materials are being used in your brand).

- Store food and pack lunches in #1, #2, #4, or #5 plastic containers, which are less likely to contain and leach organotin compounds. For maximum guaranteed safety, use glass or ceramics. Never use plastic of any kind in a microwave oven, even those that claim to be "microwave safe."

- Select natural fabrics like cotton or wools for clothing and home furnishings instead of synthetic materials.

Breathing Easier Indoors

FROM THE DEPTHS OF THE SEA, where its components dissolve into water, to the very edges of our atmosphere, air is everywhere. It is perhaps the most important of the Earth's many elements. Though living things also require water and food for life, their need for fresh air and the oxygen it contains is constant and immediate; we can live for days and even weeks without food or water, but without fresh air, we would perish in the blink of an eye.

We breathe approximately 12 times every minute. In a single day, the average adult inhales around 8,000 liters of air[1] or about 22 pounds. Each liter makes its way into the network of passageways in the lungs called bronchioles. Each bronchiole ends in a sac-like structure called an alveolus, and it's here that a complex chemical dance takes place. With each and every breath we take, the oxygen our cells need for fuel enters the bloodstream and the carbon dioxide wastes those same cells produce are removed from the body.

Of course, when we inhale, we're breathing more than oxygen. Air is composed of 78 percent nitrogen, 20 percent oxygen, and less than 1 percent each of argon, carbon dioxide, hydrogen, helium, krypton, xenon, methane, and ozone.[2] Increasingly in our modern world, air is composed of something else as well. That something else is pollution. This is true whether we're talking about indoor air or outdoor air. In fact, the air inside our homes is often far more polluted than the air just outside its walls.

How's the Air in There?

It comes as a shock to most people to learn that the air inside their homes is probably more polluted than the air outside. Yet EPA research has shown that indoor air usually contains more pollutants per cubic foot than outdoor air. How on earth could this be possible? After all, there aren't any diesel trucks idling in our living rooms, no ozone alerts being issued for our kitchens, and no lamps shining dimly through a blanket of bedroom smog. We can't see anything. We don't smell anything. What could be wrong?

According to the experts, the short answer is "plenty." Just take a look at these facts and figures from the front lines of the battle for fresh indoor air:

- EPA research has found that the air inside the typical house contains levels of pollutants two to five times higher than the air outside and in extreme cases can be one hundred times more polluted.[1]

- Various studies have placed the total number of contaminants found in America's indoor air at approximately 900.[2]

- In one study of volatile organic compounds, the Consumer Product Safety Commission found that while outdoor air at sampled sites contained less than 10 of these airborne chemical toxins, indoor air at those same sites contained 150.

Given that the average American spends about 90 percent of his or her time indoors, the EPA has ranked indoor air pollution as one of the top 5 environmental risks to public health. This in spite of the fact that a survey by the American Lung Association found that 87 percent of homeowners were not aware that indoor air quality was even an issue.

The Five Primary Causes of Indoor Air Pollution

Though every home is different, poor indoor air quality has five basic causes. Almost all instances of indoor air pollution are the result of some combination of any or all of the following factors:

1. **The chemical substances we use to clean and maintain our homes and ourselves.** Many homeowners use a large number of petrochemical cleaners, synthetic personal care items, and other toxic products like pesticides, disinfectants, and air deodorizers at home. These products spread hazardous fumes and compounds around the house and leave residues behind that gradually dissolve into the air over time. The constant use of such a wide variety of chemical compounds throughout the average home greatly increases both the number and concentration of dangerous indoor air pollutants.

   A recent study of household products by the National Environmental Trust examined toxic chemical tracking data from the states of New Jersey and Massachusetts and found that a wide variety of these products contain carcinogenic substances, reproductive and developmental poisons, and neurotoxins. For every pound of these compounds that is released into the air, water, or soil during manufacturing, an incredible 42 pounds are put into consumer products and released inside our homes.[3]

2. **The materials we use to build and furnish our homes.** Modern residences contain a staggering variety of synthetic materials from carpets and foam cushions to insulation and chemically treated pressed wood products. Many of these products outgas, which means that the chemical compounds they contain break down over time and are slowly released into the air in the form of toxic fumes. This process is also called off-gassing, and it tends to level off over time with newer materials generally emitting greater quantities of toxins than older materials. For example, the half-life for formaldehyde off-gassing from urea-formaldehyde foam insulation is two to three years. (Experts, by the way, consider this to be one of the more extreme examples of product off-gassing longevity.) That is, after two to three years the foam will have emitted half of the formaldehyde fumes it will emit over its lifetime. Over the next two to three year period, the same foam will emit half of all the formaldehyde that remains (i.e., it will emit half of the half that's left for a total of 75 percent of its lifetime emissions. This trend of releasing half of whatever is left after every two to three years will continue until the foam ceases to release any appreciable fumes at all. (After 8 to 12 years the foam will have released nearly 94 percent of its total potential emissions.)[4]

3. **Modern construction techniques.** Following the oil shocks of the 70s, most new American homes were built with energy efficiency in mind. As a result, today's homes are better insulated and more tightly sealed than any in the past. This is good for energy conservation but bad for indoor air quality. Without a system to ensure adequate air exchanges (something most houses lack), levels of hazardous indoor air pollutants tend to rise over time in homes designed to keep drafts (i.e., fresh air) out and warm or cool air in.

4. **Household combustion equipment like furnaces, hot water heaters, and gas stoves.** If improperly maintained or vented, these devices can introduce combustion by-products into indoor air that range from particulates like soot to deadly gases like carbon monoxide.

5. **Polluted outdoor air.** Windows, doors, poorly insulated walls, and drafty construction all allow outdoor air to make its way inside. While this air is often less polluted than the air already present indoors, any contaminants it does contain are frequently added to a home's existing burden of air pollution. In the absence of any wholesale "rinsing" of indoor air that occurs when windows and doors are flung wide open to allow complete air exchanges, these outdoor pollutants tend to concentrate indoors over time. This is particularly true in urban homes which are often near automobile traffic, dry cleaning operations, and other polluting activities common in developed areas.

41

Something in the Air
The Most Common Indoor Air Pollutants

What kinds of materials can get into your home's air? More than you might think! As we've seen, some 900 different pollutants have been found in indoor air. Here's a list of the most common kinds and categories of indoor air pollutants and the places they come from:

- **Carbon Monoxide** is an invisible, odorless, and tasteless gas produced by the incomplete burning of carbon-based fuels like gas and oil in devices like furnaces, gas ranges, and non-electric space and hot water heaters.

- **Combustion by-products (CBPs)** are gases and particles created by cigarette smoking, fireplaces, woodstoves, furnaces, gas ranges, and non-electric space and hot water heaters.

- **Dust** is being made around us all the time as the materials we use in our daily lives break down and shed microscopic particles. Believe it or not, the average 6-room home accumulates roughly 40 pounds of dust each year, and there's not much we can do about it. Household dust can contain tiny pieces of textiles, wood, and food; mold spores; pollens; insect fragments; furs and hairs; and particles of smoke, paint, nylon, rubber, fiberglass, plastic, and paper. (See Chapter 28 for more about dust.)

- **Formaldehyde** is a chemical used in everything from carpet and pressed wood products like plywood to bed linens. Formaldehyde is a volatile organic compound, and it's so common that some experts believe it to be the single most important indoor air pollutant. For this reason, it warrants a separate mention among the many hundreds of VOCs that can exist in indoor air. Formaldehyde is a colorless gas with a sharp odor, although at the concentrations typically found in indoor air, it is undetectable by our sense of smell. Leading sources of formaldehyde include the resins and glues found in paneling, doors, furniture, wallboard, ceiling panels, and pressed-wood products like particleboard and plywood. Other sources include carpets, decorative wallpapers, and fabrics in which formaldehyde is used as a finish to create permanent press, flame-resistant, water-repellant, and shrink-proof materials. Formaldehyde can also come from gas stoves, glues, room deodorizers, cosmetics, personal care products, paper grocery bags, waxed paper, paper tissues and towels, and even feminine protection products.

- **Nitric Oxide and Nitrogen Dioxide (Nitrogen Oxides)** are colorless, odorless, and tasteless gases produced by gas ranges.

- **Ozone** is a gas created by the breakdown of volatile compounds found in solvents; by reactions between sunlight and chemicals that are produced by burning fossil fuels; and by reactions between chemicals found in materials like paint and hair spray. Most ozone in the home comes from outside, predominantly from automobile exhaust. For this reason, ozone is more problematic in urban and suburban homes. Ozone can also come from copy machines, laser printers, and ultraviolet lights.

- **Particulates** are tiny particles of soot and other materials. The biggest sources of indoor particulates are windblown dust from outside, house dust, and tobacco smoke. Secondary sources include wood stoves and appliances like furnaces and non-electric heaters.

- **Pesticides** are chemicals intentionally designed to kill. Whether sprayed or applied in other forms, pesticides easily become airborne and can spread throughout the house far past the point of actual use, polluting both the home and its occupants.

- **Radon** is a natural radioactive gas that seeps from the rocks and soil surrounding certain homes. Radon is odorless, colorless, and tasteless and largely a problem only in basements in regions where soils have a large radon content.

- **Tobacco smoke** is a mixture of over 4,700 different chemical compounds and the single most preventable indoor air pollutant on this list.

- **Volatile Organic Compounds** are carbon-based compounds that form vapors at room temperature. In the home, the presence of these chemicals in the air comes predominantly from two sources: the outgassing of synthetic materials like foams and plastics and the use of toxic cleaning products and other household chemicals. Common VOCs include benzene, toluene, xylene, vinyl chloride, naphthalene, methylene chloride, and perchloroethylene. But such materials are just the tip of the VOC iceberg. There are hundreds of VOCs capable of causing all kinds of illnesses and ailments.

42

Indoor Air Repair

How can you tell if your home's air contains any of these pollutants? The short answer is that often you can't. That's because, with few exceptions, most indoor air pollutants have little or no smell, and those that do smell often go largely unnoticed thanks to a phenomenon known as olfactory fatigue. This is a fancy name for the fact that the nose almost immediately adapts to the presence of new odors and quickly removes them from conscious notice. In essence, your nose naturally becomes so used to most odors so fast that you cease to smell them within minutes.

In her book, *Home Safe Home,* healthy home expert Debra Lynn Dadd advises spending a long day away from home in the cleanest air you can find in order to "cleanse" your olfactory senses of this fatigue. Close windows and doors while you're out to concentrate any odors and take a big sniff immediately upon returning home. In this way you may be able to detect odors that indicate problems. Having a friend come over for a quick whiff can help too, especially if long-term exposure to your home's smells has caused long-term olfactory fatigue.[1]

Much better assessments can be obtained by indoor air quality tests. These tests usually cost between $60-80 dollars, and can be performed by homeowners without much trouble. More precise testing still can be done by a professional air quality testing firm though, it should be noted, at considerably more expense. An effective alternative strategy is to examine your home for potential sources of indoor air pollution and remove or fix any that you find.

Below is a 33-question test that highlights the typical sources of indoor air pollution in the average home. You can use it to determine whether or not your home is likely to be experiencing air quality issues.

The Seventh Generation Indoor Air Quality Test

1. Does my home have unusual and/or lingering odors?

2. Does my home regularly have stale or stuffy air?

3. Does anyone in my house smoke indoors or do I regularly have guests who smoke indoors?

4. Does anyone in my household suffer frequent colds, allergies, respiratory problems, or burning eyes?

5. Is my central heating and cooling equipment dirty or not working properly?

6. Is my fireplace or woodstove malfunctioning or improperly vented?

7. Are any of my home's various flue pipes, vents, or chimneys damaged in any way?

8. Am I using carbon-based fuels like fuel oil and propane in unvented or improperly vented devices like stoves, furnaces, and water heaters?

9. Do I use kerosene or other non-electric space heaters?

10. Does my home regularly experience high humidity?

11. Are mold or mildew present in any room?

12. Does my basement have a radon problem?

13. Does my home contain any ceiling panels, acoustic ceiling tiles, or similar products?

14. Does my home contain any ultraviolet lights?

15. Does my home contain any copy machines or computer laser printers?

16. Does my home contain any decorative wallpaper less than one year old?

17. Has my home been remodeled or added onto in the last two years?

18. Is my home weatherized or otherwise sealed tightly to conserve energy?

19. Does my home contain any plywood less than two years old?

20. Does my home contain any new furniture or carpeting less than one year old?

21. Has my home had any furniture or fixtures like cabinetry added to it in the past two years that are made from pressed or composite woods?

22. Has my home been recently painted or have any furnishings been recently painted or varnished?

23. Does my home typically accumulate a lot of dust that requires regular removal?

24. Do I use any synthetic chemical household cleaners?

25. Do I use any room deodorizers and/or air freshening products?

26. Do I use hair spray or other synthetic personal care products, especially spray products, perfumes, and nail polish supplies?

27. Do I use any pesticides, herbicides, fungicides, or other poisons inside or outside my home?

28. Does anyone in the house engage in hobbies or other activities that make frequent use of adhesives like rubber cement or model glue, strippers, finishes, paints, wood fillers, etc.?

29. Do I have any textile products labeled permanent press, easy-care, wrinkle-free, flame-resistant, etc. that are less than one year old?

30. Does my home contain any synthetic foams?

31. Do I use dry cleaning services regularly?

32. Is my home located on or near any heavily traveled roads?

33. Is my home located near any commercial facilities that emit air hazards, like a dry cleaner, car repair or body shop, factory, etc.

If you answered "yes" to any of the above questions, the chances are good that your home could use some remedial action. The more affirmative answers you gave, the greater that action likely needs to be and the faster it probably should happen. If you find yourself unsure about how to answer any of the questions, consider that your cue to learn more about your home via professional testing, inspections, and your own explorations in order to find out whether it has any unknown sources of indoor air pollution.

Even if you answered "no" to every item on our test, coming up with a perfect score that indicates your home is probably free of indoor air quality problems, it's wise to adopt a few principles of healthy precaution to keep things that way.

There are two overarching strategies you can adopt to clean up your home's air. First and most importantly, try to eliminate all potential sources of indoor air pollution in your home (see our above test for areas to think about). This is the single most effective strategy to ensure a safe supply of indoor air. Elimination of an air pollution source means its pollution is gone forever. You won't have to worry about it, monitor it, or deal with it in any way, and your air will be that much cleaner permanently.

Secondly, ventilate your home. Ventilation brings in fresh air from the outdoors to dilute and replace the air trapped inside your house. Opening doors and windows and using window and exhaust fans whenever possible can go a long way toward restoring healthy indoor air. However, ventilation is not without its limitations. The air outside may itself contain high levels of some pollutants, especially in more urbanized areas. Also, the weather and temperature outdoors may not permit the long periods of air exchange generally needed for maximum effect. Still, any amount of ventilation, no matter how small, is usually helpful. And the healthier indoor conditions this ventilation creates is generally worth any increased heating or cooling costs that result from a home thrown open to the great outdoors for that purpose.

43

A Room-by-Room Guide to Better Breathing

In addition to these general ideas, the following more specific strategies will go a long way toward the goal of healthy indoor air. Keep in mind, however, that complete removal of all indoor air pollution sources will be difficult unless you're willing to forgo a variety of modern conveniences and materials. In addition, some of the tips listed here involve things like renovations that are beyond the immediate reach of most of us. For these and other reasons, controlling indoor air pollution is in many ways a long-term project. You may not be willing or able, for example, to replace the pressed wood cabinetry in your home next week. But when the time for replacement does eventually arrive somewhere down the road, you can seize the opportunity to make a further positive difference in your home's air quality. Whether you decide to tackle one or all of the steps listed here, remember that every action you take will result in air that's cleaner and healthier for you and your family to breathe.

Around the House

- Grow a lot of plants. Houseplants act as natural air filters that remove pollutants and keep indoor atmospheres cleaner. (See page 159 for more on houseplants.)

- Do not use urea-formaldehyde insulation when and if you renovate or reinsulate.

- If you smoke, stop immediately. Forbid smoking in your house or even on its grounds. If this is too challenging, use a HEPA air filter whenever smokers are present. Make sure the filter you choose for the job includes activated carbon post-filtration and offers a high air exchange rate.

- If you use a humidifier, clean it frequently with a strong solution of vinegar and water.

- Clean air conditioners and check for mold or bacteria growth inside. Change their filters regularly.

- Avoid furniture and fixtures made from particleboard, plywood, and other composite wood materials.

- If you get new furniture or carpeting that isn't made from 100 percent natural materials, air these items out before you bring them into your home. Both furnishings and carpets can and do contain a wide variety of chemical compounds that release toxic fumes slowly over time in a process called out-gassing. Place furnishings in the garage for a few weeks before adding them to your home. Similarly, leave rolls of carpet unrolled or loosely rolled in the garage for a similar amount time. (Even better, tell the dealer to air it out at his or her warehouse prior to delivery.) Since outgassing decreases over time and is most serious when a product is brand new, these actions will reduce the levels of hazardous fumes to which your family will be exposed. By the same token, don't accept carpets treated with stain repellents, mildewcides, or other chemicals. Don't install carpets with adhesives, a key source of formaldehyde gas. Instead, use mechanical means like tacks. Once you install carpet, keep fresh air circulating through the room for a year to clean air of any out-gassing still occurring.

- If you have a laser printer or a photocopier, place and use these devices in a well-ventilated space. Turn them on only when they're actually being used.

In the Kitchen

- If you have a gas range make sure the flames are blue (an indication of complete combustion). Orange flames should be adjusted.

- All gas ranges should have a ventilation hood that sends air outside and is located away from windows and doors. If you don't have a hood, open the nearest window while cooking.

- Never use a gas range as a heat source.

- When buying a new gas range, don't purchase one with a pilot light.

- Use a chlorine-free dishwasher detergent. The chlorine found in both treated water supplies and traditional dishwasher detergents is volatized, or turned to vapors, by hot dishwasher water. Dishwasher steam is routinely released during or after each washing cycle and whenever it is the vaporized chlorine it contains and the volatized chlorinated hydrocarbons it produces are added to indoor air. (See Chapter 25 for more on dishwasher dilemmas.)

In the Living Room

- If you're buying a woodstove, choose one with a catalytic converter or secondary combustion chamber. These reduce hydrocarbon gas and particulate emissions.
- Periodically check stovepipe joints and gaskets to make sure they're sealed properly.
- Have your fireplace and/or wood stove cleaned and inspected annually.
- Vent all gas or kerosene heaters to the outside.
- Whenever possible, opt for natural fiber stuffings instead of synthetic foams in sofas, chairs, and other furnishings.

In the Basement

- Test your basement for radon.
- Have your furnace and hot water heater cleaned and inspected annually. If your furnace is a forced air type, change its air filters every other month.
- Install a ventilating heat exchanger (these let you ventilate your home without the loss of any warm or cool air it contains).

In the Bathroom

- Ventilate bathrooms well and often.
- To reduce or prevent mold and mildew, wipe fixtures and walls clean frequently. Keep them as free of standing moisture as possible.
- Do not use hair spray.
- If your home's water supply is treated with chlorine, install a showerhead filter that removes this hazardous chemical. This will prevent chlorine volatized by hot shower water into vapors from entering the air.
- Don't use synthetic personal care products.

In the Bedroom

- Change bedroom linens frequently — as often as two to three times a week when humidity is high — in order to fight dust mites.

- Use only non-petroleum candles with cloth wicks and natural essential oil scents. Synthetically scented paraffin and other synthetic wax candles emit unhealthy fumes and soot when burned. Beeswax and vegetable waxes produce less. Make sure any wick you light does not contain a thin metal strand to help it stand upright. Though a recent Consumer Products Safety Commission decision finally banned deadly lead from reinforced wicks, lead-containing products will remain on store shelves for some time. (And the zinc and tin substitutes that replace them aren't the best things to be breathing either!)

Cleaning Up

- Do not use chlorine bleach or products containing it. Be aware that chlorine hides inside ingredients like sodium hypochlorite, cyanuric chloride, and other chemicals that have "chlor" in their names.

- Do not use air fresheners or room deodorizers.

- Do not use any synthetic chemical-based household cleaning products.

- Clean your home as frequently as possible with naturally based products or materials. Dust with a very slightly damp cloth instead of a dry one.

- Vacuum upholstered furniture.

- Use a HEPA vacuum or one that offers enhanced filtration of its exhaust.

- Have your carpets and rugs professionally steam-cleaned once a year. Make sure only detergent-free steam is used and don't maintain rugs between these cleanings with any kind of chemical cleaning product.

- Groom pets regularly and outdoors if possible. Do not use chemical flea collars, repellents, or treatments.

Out and About

- Do not use pesticides. Ever.

- Tightly seal partially used paints, solvents, strippers, and other chemical products and store them in a well-ventilated area as far away from the living areas of your home as possible. As soon as you can, take these products to a hazardous waste collection site.

- If you have an attached garage, do not leave your car running inside it for any period of time.

44

Air vs. Machine
Cleaning Your Air With Filters and Purifiers

Another strategy that can make indoor air healthier is the use of air purification devices. These machines use a variety of different mechanical methods to scrub the air inside your home free of pollutants. Many people prefer to rely exclusively, or nearly so, on air purifiers to keep their home's air clean because of the sheer simplicity of such a solution. However, this strategy is imperfect at best for several reasons.

First, though air purifiers certainly make air cleaner, no single machine or technology can eliminate 100 percent of all pollutants present 100 percent of the time. Instead, each has its own set of limitations that can range from an inability to remove certain contaminants to an airflow that may not be able to keep up with the particular sources of pollution in your home. Air purifiers also use energy and require frequent maintenance. For these reasons, they're best used as a supplement to strategies that seek to actually eliminate indoor air pollution at its source rather than as a solution in and of themselves.

When selecting an air purifier, the following things should be considered:

- What pollutants you want to remove from your air and the effectiveness of the filter in handling them

- The size of the area you want cleaned

- The cost of the device relative to the above needs

- The amount of noise a filter will make

- What maintenance will be required to keep the device performing at top efficiency.[1]

Here is a look at the different air purification devices and technologies available for home use:

Activated carbon filters work by a process called adsorption in which pollutants are attracted to the microscopic pores naturally present in highly carbonized materials like charcoal.[2] Activated carbon has been treated with steam to enhance this natural porosity and create as many additional pores as possible. This process gives the carbon a tremendous surface area capable of great filtering ability.[3] To be effective, a carbon filter should be at least one inch thick.[4] Carbon filters should also be changed regularly. Research has shown that carbon can trap contaminants when they are present at high levels but will then slowly release them back into clean air over time.[5] Changing the carbon filter media every few months will help cut down on this re-release of pollutants.

Activated carbon filters will remove pesticides, some nitrogen oxides, phenols, some sulphur dioxide, tobacco smoke gases, ozone, and many organic chemicals.[6] Activated carbon filters are also adept at removing some but not all VOCs and other gases. Many VOCs with smaller molecules will pass through carbon. For this reason, some activated carbon filters are enhanced with other materials to trap one or more specific VOCs. If VOCs are a concern in your home, check any prospective filters carefully before making your purchase to ensure that the carbon they contain has been treated to remove the necessary VOCs.

Unenhanced activated carbon filters will not remove particles like asbestos dust, pollens, molds, animal dander, and tobacco smoke particles.[7]

HEPA filters were originally developed by the Atomic Energy Commission to remove radioactive plutonium particles from the air in nuclear labs,[8] HEPA stands for "High Efficiency Particulate Arresting." For the most part, these filters consist of pollutant-trapping polyester or fiberglass fibers held together by resins.[9] These fibers create a maze of tiny passageways whose twists and turns are able to trap many air contaminants.

By law, HEPA filters must earn their designation by trapping 99.97 of all particles down to 0.3 microns in size.[10] Interestingly, unlike many filters, HEPA filters actually become more effective over time. As they trap more and more pollutants, their increasingly clogged passageways become smaller, which enables them to trap even more particles. Eventually, however, the efficiency level of a HEPA filter will plateau and then decline necessitating a filter change.

Highly sensitive individuals should note that the synthetic materials used in HEPA filters may create odors or other objectionable effects. An activated carbon post-filter can help reduce these.[11] Additionally, an active carbon post-filter will capture many of the air pollutants HEPA alone cannot. *In general, the most effective home air filters consist of a HEPA/activated carbon combination.*

HEPA filters alone will remove particulates like asbestos, dust, pollen, mold, animal dander, and tobacco smoke particles. They will also remove bacteria and viruses.[12] HEPA filters alone will not remove gases like VOCs, carbon monoxide, nitrogen oxides, ozone, sulphur dioxide, and tobacco smoke gases. They are also ineffective against pesticides and other organic chemicals.

Electrostatic filters harness electrostatic force to clean indoor air. These filters use a special plastic media that becomes negatively charged with static electricity as air passes through them. (Some electrostatic filters have a permanent built-in charge.) This negatively charged surface attracts and holds positively charged pollutants carried in on entering air.[13] Most electrostatic filters are designed to be used in a central forced air heating or cooling system. Because not all air pollutants have a positive charge, electrostatic filters have a limited ability to clean air.[14] They will capture molds, pollens, and many particulates like asbestos, animal dander, and tobacco smoke particles.[15] They will not remove any gases in the air.

Electrostatic precipitators use a principle similar to electrostatic filters, but don't require air to pass through a filter media in order to clean it.[16] Unlike electrostatic filters, they use electricity to generate their negative charges. This electricity passes through large metal wires and imparts a strong negative electric charge to passing pollutants, which are then collected on a series of positively charged plates. These plates must be regularly cleaned as contaminants will quickly build up on their surfaces, reducing their efficiency. Most can be cleaned in a dishwasher or simply washed in the sink.[17]

If you buy an electrostatic precipitator make sure it has these collection plates. Some do not and work by negatively charging pollutants and forcing them back into the room where they are drawn to the positive charges on room surfaces. Gradually, these become soiled with accumulated contaminants. These deposited pollutants can be reintroduced to the air during cleaning, and the cleaning itself can be quite a chore since it will now involve walls and ceilings as well as drapes and other surfaces.[18] Electrostatic precipitators are usually only 80 percent efficient (that is they trap only 80 percent of the particles they are theoretically capable of capturing) and this efficiency can quickly drop to 20 percent as collection plates become dirty. They may also introduce unhealthy ozone into your air.[19]

Electrostatic precipitators will capture molds, pollens, and particulates like asbestos, animal dander, and tobacco smoke particles, but will not remove any gases present in the air.[20]

Ion generators are a type of electrostatic precipitator. They work by releasing negatively charged ions into the air. These ions attract positively charged pollutants and transfer their charge to them. Some ion generators have a positively charged collection plate to

attract these negatively charged contaminants. But others do not, and in these cases pollutants will deposit themselves onto room surfaces, which will require cleaning.[21] For this
reason, a collection plate system is recommended.

Ion generators have a limited cleaning ability. They will not do much to affect levels of
pollen or dust and generally will remove only small particles. But they are highly efficient
at cleaning indoor air of smog and tobacco smoke-related particulates. Ion generators will
not remove gases of any kind.[22] Ion generators also offer a healthy side effect in the form
of the negative ions they produce. There is some evidence indicating that negative ions can
create a feeling of well-being, produce greater mental and physical energy, bring relief
from allergies and asthma, promote faster healing of wounds, and reduce pain for burn victims and sufferers of chronic conditions.[23]

Ozone generators are the most controversial of all of today's air cleaning devices.
They work by creating ozone, a form of highly reactive oxygen. Ozone is an extremely
powerful oxidizer capable of destroying many of the air contaminants with which it comes
into contact. However, ozone is also itself a dangerous pollutant that can irritate skin, eyes,
and mucous membranes, cause breathing problems, and even damage household furnishings. Unfortunately, the line between "good" levels of ozone (i.e., those that are okay for
people but bad for pollutants) and "bad" levels of ozone (i.e., those that are bad for people and everything else) is a very fine one. It doesn't take much ozone in indoor air for
unhealthy levels to be achieved. In fact, it's so potent that just a little too much can create
a hazardous condition.

Ozone generators can usually be adjusted up or down to control both the amount of
ozone emitted and the frequency of these emissions. It is extremely important to adjust
them properly to avoid unhealthy ozone levels in indoor air. Unfortunately, many ozone
generators have complicated controls which make this difficult to do. It's also difficult if
not impossible to verify that an ozone generator is operating properly and releasing the
desired amount of ozone. Any space containing an ozone generator should be ventilated
frequently to prevent ozone build-up.

Ozone is highly effective at destroying bacteria and viruses, and removing odors from
the air. It will also break down certain VOCs into less harmful compounds. However,
ozone is also capable of reacting with existing air pollutants to create new pollutants that
weren't previously present.[24]

Because of their frequently complicated controls and instructions, the difficulty in veri-
fying proper performance, and the inherent health hazards of even small excesses in indoor
ozone levels, indoor air quality experts do not recommend these devices for consumer use.

45

Air Fresheners Stink

If one thing is certain in our uncertain world, it's that there's no shortage of odors in the modern home. From dinner gone wrong to pets gone unwashed, there's usually something funky fouling up the domestic olfactory landscape and wrinkling our sensitive noses in the process. No wonder air freshener sales in the US rose 43 percent between 1998 and 2003.[1] These products effortlessly cover up odorous offenses. No fuss. Just fragrance. That and some serious health hazards of which few users are aware.

In general, air fresheners don't remove odors. They simply use chemicals to cover them up. In some cases, they even work by employing chemicals that reduce the ability of the nose to smell. Since air fresheners do nothing to stop the source of offensive odors, those odors remain in the air and the product must be reapplied frequently, which increases your exposure to the chemicals they contain.

Many of these chemicals either have a dubious safety record or remain untested for human health effects. Toxins found in air fresheners and room deodorizers include naphthalene, phenol, cresol, dichlorobenzene, and xylene among many others. Air freshener chemicals have been implicated in cancer, neurological damage, reproductive and developmental disorders, and other conditions. The compounds in air fresheners, particularly the synthetic fragrances they contain, can also aggravate asthma or trigger attacks.

Pinene and limonene are two common chemicals found in those air freshening units that plug into electrical sockets and automatically release aromatic compounds over time. Both easily react with ozone, a common indoor air pollutant, to create formaldehyde and a variety of related chemicals that have been implicated in respiratory conditions.

For these reasons, indoor air quality experts recommend against using air fresheners or room deodorizers of any kind. Rather than clean your home's air, most actually make it more dangerous to breathe. Instead of chemicals, try these safe methods to freshen the air in your home:

- Use natural minerals like baking soda and borax to control common odor sources and to deodorize when you clean.

≈ Indoor air quality experts recommend against using air fresheners or room deodorizers of any kind. ≈

- Locate sources of odors and eliminate them whenever and wherever possible. Since many odors are the result of microbial action, spraying trouble spots and potentially problematic areas (like trash cans, compost containers, etc.) with a three percent solution of hydrogen peroxide (the concentration typically available in stores) will remove many problems.

- Keep windows open as much as possible to let bad air out and good air in. If odors are still troubling, try an air purifier with activated carbon filtration.

- To scent indoor air, place a drop of a natural essential oil like lavender or mint on a light bulb, or add a dozen drops to a bowl of water placed on a radiator. You can also boil fragrant dried herbs in a pot of water to release a fresh smell.

- A natural mineral called zeolite is available in packets that will absorb odors when hung in problem areas like musty basements and closets.

- Make your own sprays from essential oils and other safe, natural ingredients. For recipes and more information, we recommend the book *Better Basics for the Home* (see the Resource Guide).

46

Use the Power of Plants to Grow
a Healthy Harvest of Cleaner Air

During the Skylab III mission in 1973, NASA scientists realized they had a serious problem. The space age materials they'd used to build their space age space station were emitting hazardous fumes and polluting the facility's tightly sealed air supply. Studies of the problem identified over 300 different volatile organic compounds in the spacecraft's atmosphere, and while there were no immediate effects on the health of the astronauts living there, the findings had clear implications for the permanent outpost then being planned for the moon. Researchers were rightfully worried that moon base residents exposed to such extensive air pollution for long periods of time would eventually become ill.

To find an answer to their interplanetary dilemma, NASA planners turned to the earth for inspiration. Our planet, of course, uses its plant life to clean and recharge its atmosphere. In the simplest terms, it's bad air in and good air out. With this in mind, agency scientists set about seeing if they could replicate these natural purification processes. They built a series of sealed chambers, placed houseplants inside, and injected formaldehyde, a typical indoor air pollutant. In 1984, published study results revealed that the plants were, in fact, able to remove this hazardous VOC from their chambers' air. A subsequent two-year study conducted by NASA and the Associated Landscape Contractors of America examined the ability of 12 types of plants to remove formaldehyde, benzene, and trichloroethylene. Results were again positive, and a new environmental strategy was born, one that used ordinary houseplants to create cleaner and healthier indoor air.[1]

Scientists have since discovered that houseplants contribute to healthy air in a variety of ways. Both houseplant soils and leaves emit relatively large amounts of water vapor that help keep indoor air properly humidified. Plants also give off compounds called phyto-chemicals that actually work to suppress mold spores and bacteria in indoor air, a mechanism researchers believe has evolved as a defense against airborne microbes. Studies have shown that the atmosphere in rooms filled with houseplants typically contains between 50 percent to 60 percent fewer mold spores and bacteria.

The real power of plants, however, lies in their ability to remove unhealthy chemicals from our indoor air. Houseplants excel at removing VOCs and other gaseous compounds from indoor air. (Note, however, that they won't help with other indoor air hazards like particulates, dust, radon, etc.) Plants accomplish this task in two main ways. The first is by absorbing chemicals in the air via microscopic leaf openings called stomata. Once a pollutant has been absorbed, the plant either breaks it down or sends it down to the plant's roots. There it's released as food for the colonies of symbiotic microbes that typically live in a plant's root zone. Pollutants are also removed from the air and delivered to soil bacteria by a mechanism known as transpiration. In this process, the water vapor a plant emits through its leaves rises away from the plant and into the atmosphere. This creates convection currents of air that move in the opposite direction toward the base of the plant, drawing pollutants into the soil where they're rendered harmless.

≈ The atmosphere in rooms filled with houseplants typically contains between 50 percent to 60 percent fewer mold spores and bacteria. ≈

Using plants to help purify indoor air requires more than a few houseplants. Homes with indoor air problems as well as healthy homes seeking to stay that way won't be able to accomplish their aims with a handful of potted plants on a windowsill. On the other hand, it's by no means necessary to live in a jungle in order to get cleaner and healthier indoor air. Placing houseplants in reasonable abundance throughout the home will result in a healthier atmosphere than that found in a home where no plants are present at all.

Because the amounts and types of individual pollutants removed by plants differ from species to species, and because the levels of specific pollutants often vary significantly from home to home, there's no set number of plants recommended by experts for maximum results. Instead, the general rule of thumb is "the more plants, the healthier the air." This purification power can be maximized by choosing those plants found to have the greatest air cleaning abilities. Following is a list of 20 of the top choices for removing gaseous pollutants from indoor air.[2] Exceptional abilities are noted where applicable.

The Top 20 Air-Purifying Plants

1. Boston fern *(Nephrolepis exaltata Bostoniensis)*. This is the number one plant in overall purifying performance.

2. Areca palm *(Chyrsalidocarpus lutescens)*. Another top overall performer.

3. Lady palm *(Rhapis excelsa)*.

4. Bamboo palm *(Chamaedorea seifrizii)*. One of the top rated plants for removing formaldehyde, benzene and trichloroethylene. Also noted for high transpiration rates.

5. Rubber plant *(Ficus robusta)*. Excels at removing formaldehyde.

6. Dracaena Janet Craig *(Dracaena deremensis)*. Excels at removing formaldehyde.

7. English Ivy *(Hedera helix)*. Excels at removing formaldehyde.

8. Dwarf date palm *(Phoenix roebelenii)*. Especially recommended for removing xylene.

9. Ficus alii *(Ficus macleilandii alii)*.

10. Peace lily *(Spathiphyllum sp.)*. Excellent for removing alcohols, acetone, formaldehyde, benzene, and trichloroethylene.

11. Corn plant *(Dracaena fragrans Massangeana)*. Another good choice for removing formaldehyde.

12. Golden pothos *(Epipremnum aureum)*.

13. Kimberly queen fern *(Nephrolepis obliterata)*. Good for removing formaldehyde and alcohols.

14. Florists mum *(Chrysanthemum morifolium)*. A good seasonal choice for removing formaldehyde, benzene, and ammonia.

15. Gerbera daisy *(Gerbera jamesonii)*. Has a high transpiration rate.

16. Dracaena warneckei *(Dracaena deremensis warneckei)*. Excels at removing benzene.

17. Dragon tree *(Dracaena marginata)*. A top choice for removing xylene and trichloroethylene.

18. Schefflera *(Brassaia actinophylla)*.

19. Spider plant *(Chlorophytum comosum)*.

20. Weeping fig *(Ficus benjamina)*.

47

Ending Bad Air Days One Breath at a Time

Are you finding yourself a bit breathless just thinking about all the work that needs to be done in order to assure your family of a clean and healthy air supply at home? Breathe deep and relax! Cleaning up a home's air and keeping it that way is neither complicated nor difficult. Just remember two simple ideas along the way:

1. Very few if any homes contain every source of indoor air pollution and all the potential contaminants it's possible to find. In fact, in most homes it's just the opposite: there are just a few sources of serious indoor air problems and only a handful of pollutants present in quantities large enough to cause ongoing concern. Healing the air in the average home is simply a matter of zeroing in on these sources and pollutants and repairing or removing them.

2. And that's something each of us can only do one task at a time. Like the overall proposition of creating a healthier home, remaking your home's atmosphere isn't something anyone expects you to start and finish overnight. Instead, it's an evolutionary process that takes you in small steps toward some big goals. Focus on one source or pollutant at a time. Tackle something here and another thing there. Take care of big ticket items like cabinet replacement or a new furnace as budgets permit. Keep going and keep doing, and slowly but surely, you'll fill your home with a breath of fresh air that's healthy for everyone to breathe.

Recommended Products

IN AN EFFORT TO FIND THOSE PRODUCTS that posed the least risk to you and the environment, we evaluated three hundred cleaning products. We looked at ingredients listed on the labels. We scoured the web and looked at MSDS sheets. If we still didn't have a complete ingredient list, we called the manufacturer and asked them to provide one. Once we had a list of ingredients, we evaluated their risk.

In this section, we turn the results of those investigations into a list of the household cleaning products that we recommend, and provide a detailed look at the ingredients that make these products safer for your family and healthier for your home.

We considered:

Acute toxicity: The product's ability to cause immediate harm. No recommended products contain an ingredient that is highly toxic as defined by the Consumer Product Safety Commission.

Chronic toxicity: The product's ability to cause harm after many years of use. No recommended products contain an ingredient that is highly irritating or a skin sensitizer as defined by the Consumer Product Safety Commission.

Ecotoxicity: The product's ability to readily biodegrade; its ability to cause harm to the aquatic environment. All ingredients in recommended products are readily biodegradable as determined by European Union test 301 and have a low aquatic toxicity.

After applying these criteria to all the products we evaluated, only 35 made the list. These products were the crème-de-la-crème. There were other products that had real environmental benefits but which did meet all our criteria. For example, phosphate-free automatic dishwasher detergents that contained a non-toxic but non-biodegradable polymer were excluded from this list. Even though such products are much more desirable than conventional products, they did not meet our stringent requirements and so are not included.

The list of 35 recommended products, including their ingredients and toxicity ratings, is found in Table 1.

None of the recommended products were tested for performance. Recommendation of a product is based solely on its ingredients and does not represent an endorsement of the product's performance.

All recommended products are composed of plant-derived ingredients that are readily biodegradable, and mineral ingredients.

In each category, each ingredient was considered as A — posing no or little risk, B — posing minimal risk, or C — posing moderate or high risk. No products rating a C in any category were recommended.

A complete list of the evaluation criteria is found in Table 2.

After creating our list of Recommended Products, we looked at the ingredients used and created a list of those ingredients. Of course, there are many other ingredients that are not acutely or chronically toxic, and that have only a minimal impact on the environment. However, we did not want to create such a list here. Rather, we are just reporting what some well formulated products contained.

The list of ingredients is found in Table 3.

Table 1 — Recommended Products

Products	TOXICITY[1]						Ingredients
	ACUTE		CHRONIC			ENV	
	Irritants	Allergens & Strong Sensitizers	Carcinogens	Neurotoxins	Reproductive Effects	Biodegradability	
LIQUID LAUNDRY DETERGENTS							
Life Tree® Original Premium Laundry Liquid	B[4]	A	B[5a]	A	A	A	alcohol ethoxylate, APG, tall oil fatty acid, cocamidopropyl betaine, essential oil fragrance blend
Seventh Generation® Laundry Liquid — Free & Clear	B[4]	A	B[5a]	A	B[5b]	A	alcohol ethoxylate, SLES, APG, borax, sodium gluconate, sodium chloride, sodium hydroxide, protease enzyme, amylase enzyme, calcium chloride, preservative Kathon CG
Seventh Generation® borax,Laundry Liquid — scented	B[4]	A	B[5a]	A	B[5b]	A	alcohol ethoxylate, SLES, APG, sodium gluconate, sodium hydroxide, sodium chloride, protease enzyme, amylase enzyme, calcium chloride, preservative Kathon CG, essential oils
Sun & Earth® Deep Cleaning Formula Laundry Detergent	B[4]	A	B[5a]	A	A	A	SLES, d-glucopyranoside, d-limonene, sodium carbonate
Seventh Generation® Sensitive Care	B[4]	A	B[5a]	A	B[5b]	A	SLES, APG, borax, sodium gluconate, preservative Kathon CG, calcium chloride, sodium citrate, sodium hydroxide, sorbitol
Seventh Generation® Baby Formula	B[4]	A	B[5a]	A	B[5b]	A	SLES, alcohol ethoxylate, APG, borax, calcium chloride, preservative Kathon CG, sodium gluconate, enzymes, sodium chloride, sodium hydroxide
LAUNDRY POWDER DETERGENTS							
Seventh Generation® Laundry Powder — all variations	B[4]	A	B[5a]	A	A	A	sodium percarbonate, alcohol ethoxylate, enzyme, carboxymethyl cellulose, sodium carbonate, citrus oil

	TOXICITY[1]						
	ACUTE		CHRONIC			ENV	
Products	Irritants	Allergens & Strong Sensitizers	Carcinogens	Neurotoxins	Reproductive Effects	Biodegradability	Ingredients
LAUNDRY ADDITIVES							
Seventh Generation® Natural Fabric Softener — Lavender	B[4]	A	A	A	A	A	quaternary amine (soy derived), preservative Kathon CG, lavender oil
Sun & Earth® Ultra Fabric Softener	B[4]	A	A	A	A	A	quaternary amine (plant derived), cocamidopropyl betaine
Ecover® Natural Fabric Softener	B[4]	A	B[5c]	A	A	A	TEA esterquaternary amine (plant derived), sorbic acid, salt, fragrance (plant derived)
Bi-O-Kleen™ Oxygen Bleach Plus (powder)	B[4]	A	A	A	A	A	grapefruit seed extract, soda ash, sodium sulfate, sodium percarbonate, zeolites
Seventh Generation® Non-Chlorine Bleach (liquid)	B[4]	A	A	A	A	A	hydrogen peroxide
Ecover® Natural Non-Chlorine Bleach Ultra (liquid)	B[4]	A	A	A	A	A	hydrogen peroxide
OXO-Brite Non-Chlorine Bleach (powder)	B[4]	A	A	A	A	A	sodium percarbonate, sodium carbonate
Bio Pac Non Chlorine Bleach Powder (powder)	B[4]	A	A	A	A	A	percarbonate, sodium chloride, sodium carbonate
Oxi Clean Multi-Purpose Stain Remover	B[4]	A	A	A	A	A	sodium percarbonate, sodium carbonate
DISHWASHING LIQUIDS							
Seventh Generation® Dish Liquid — Free & Clear	B[4]	A	B[5a, c]	A	A	A	SLES, cocamidopropyl betaine, cocamide MEA, magnesium chloride, sodium chloride, sodium citrate, preservative Kathon CG
Seventh Generation® Dish Liquid — all scents	B[4]	A	B[5a, c]	A	A	A	SLES, cocamidopropyl betaine, cocamide MEA, magnesium chloride, sodium citrate, sodium chloride, essential oils, preservative Kathon CG
Citra Solv® Ultra Citra-Dish Natural Dishwashing Liquid with Aloe	B[4]	A	A	A	A	A	ethyl alcohol, sodium chloride, orange oil

Products	TOXICITY[1] ACUTE		CHRONIC			ENV	Ingredients
	Irritants	Allergens & Strong Sensitizers	Carcinogens	Neurotoxins	Reproductive Effects	Biodegradability	
Sun & Earth® Ultra Dishwashing Liquid	B[4]	A	B5a	A	A	A	SLES, cocamidopropyl betaine, d-glucopyranoside, orange oil
AUTOMATIC DISH-WASHER DETERGENTS & RINSE AIDS							
Ecover® Rinse Aid	B[4]	A	A	A	A	A	APG, ethanol (plant derived), citric acid
GLASS CLEANERS & ALL PURPOSE SPRAY CLEANERS							
Seventh Generation® All Purpose Cleaner, Free & Clear	B[4]	A	B[5a]	A	A	A	APG, alcohol ethoxylate, sodium laurimin-odipropionate, sodium citrate, sodium carbonate, preservative Kathon CG
Seventh Generation® Citrus Cleaner & Degreaser	B[4]	A	B[5a]	A	A	A	APG, alcohol ethoxylate, sodium laurimin-odipropionate, sodium citrate, sodium carbonate, orange oil, preservative Kathon CG
Seventh Generation® Glass & Surface Cleaner, Free & Clear	B[4]	A	A	A	A	A	APG, preservative Kathon CG
Dr. Bronner's Sal Suds (All Purpose Cleaner)	B[4]	A	A	A	A	A	SLS, coco betaine, lauryl glucoside, fir needle oil, spruce oil
AIR FRESHENERS							
Earth Friendly Uni-Fresh Air Freshener — cinnamon scent	B[4]	A	B[7]	A	A	A	surfactant, plant derived, unspecified, alcohol (corn derived), essential oils
Earth Friendly Uni-Fresh Air Freshener — lavender scent	B[4]	A	B[7]	A	A	A	surfactant, plant derived, unspecified, alcohol (corn derived), essential oils
Air Scense Natural Air "Refresheners" (lavender)	B[4]	A	A	A	A	A	vanilla natural fragrance, alcohol, grain
Air Scense Natural Air "Refresheners" (orange)	B[4]	A	A	A	A	A	d-limonene, other citrus oils

TOXICITY[1]

Products	ACUTE		CHRONIC			ENV	Ingredients
	Irritants	Allergens & Strong Sensitizers	Carcinogens	Neurotoxins	Reproductive Effects	Biodegradability	
OTHER PRODUCTS							
Ecover® Natural Toilet Bowl Cleaner Thick Formula	B[4]	A	A	A	A	A	APG, citric acid, lactic acid (plant derived), xanthan gum, citrate, fragrance (plant derived)
Citra-Wood Natural Furniture Polish & Wood Replenisher	B[4]	A	A	A	A	A	soybean oil, d-limonene, soy methyl esters
Earth Friendly Earth Enzymes (drain)	B[4]	A	A	A	A	A	sodium sesquicarbonate, bacterial mixtures, proteolytic enzyme
Citra-Drain Natural Enzymatics	B[4]	A	A	A	A	A	bacteria complex
Nature's Best Plumber	B[4]	A	A	A	A	A	dried enzyme, bacterial culture

Notes: Toxicity (Acute, Chronic, Environmental)
A — Little or no risk
B — Minimal risk
C — Moderate or high risk
See Table 2: Risk Criteria for references. The reference number refers to the Issue ID.

Table 2 — Risk Criteria for Cleaning Product Ingredients

Issue ID	Issue	Comments
1	Performance	None of the recommended products were tested for performance. Recommendation of a product is based solely on its ingredients and does not represent an endorsement of the product's performance.
2	Ingredient origin	To be recommended, a product must be composed of plant-derived ingredients that are readily biodegradable, and of mineral ingredients.
3	Acute toxicity	To be recommended, no product may contain an ingredient that is highly toxic as defined by the Consumer Product Safety Commission.
4	Irritancy and sensitization	To be recommended, no product may contain an ingredient that is highly irritating or a skin sensitizer, as defined by the Consumer Product Safety Commission. All products were listed as "B — Minimal Risk" for irritancy because human chemistries are highly variable, and some individuals are always at risk. If a specific irritancy or sensitization issue was identified that raised the risk to "C — Moderate or High Risk."
5	Chronic toxicity	To be recommended, no product may contain an ingredient that is a known or probable human carcinogen, a known neurotoxin, or a known reprotoxicant. Some ingredients may contain trace levels of chronic toxicants. In these cases the appropriate chronic toxicity was identified as "B — Minimal Risk" (see Issue IDs 5a and 5c).
5a		Ethoxylated surfactants (alcohol ethoxylates and SLES) may be contaminated with 1,4-dioxane, a probable human carcinogen. Most manufacturers remove this contaminant by a process called "vacuum stripping." However, consumers are advised to confirm this with the product manufacturer.
5b		Borax has been shown to affect the reproductive vitality of test animals and borax miners. Significant levels of exposure were required to show any affect. For this reason, products that contain borax (sodium borate) were identified as "B — Minimal Risk" with respect to reproductive toxicity.
5c		Some products contain a surfactant reacted with a nitrogen-containing substance called an amine. Diethanolamine (DEA), monoethanolamine (MEA), and triethanolamine (TEA) are the amines most commonly used. DEA can react with nitrites to form a carcinogen called a nitrosamine. Thus, surfactants with DEA are not recommended. Surfactants with MEA and TEA may contain trace amounts of DEA. Thus there is a minimal risk nitrosamines may form, and these products were identified as "B — Minimal Risk."
6	Environmental toxicity	Ingredients must be readily biodegradable as determined by EU test 301, and must not have a high aquatic toxicity.
7	Unspecified Surfactant	Plant oils must be modified to be effective surfactants. An unspecified, plant-derived surfactant may be ethoxylated or reacted with an amine, and thus these products were identified as "B — Minimal Risk."

Table 3 — Ingredients Used in Recommended Products

Issue

ID	Issue	Comments
1		
2	Alcohol ethoxylate, plant derived, unspecified (ethoxylated alcohol)	A biodegradable nonionic surfactant made from a plant fatty alcohol (such as lauryl alcohol) and ethylene oxide. Alcohol ethoxylates may be contaminated with 1,4-dioxane, a probable human carcinogen. However, most companies remove 1,4-dioxane contamination by a process called vacuum stripping.
3	Alkyl polyglycoside (APG)	A mild, biodegradable nonionic surfactant derived from cornstarch and a plant fatty alcohol (such as lauryl alcohol). Found in: detergents, hand dish soap, all purpose cleaners, and hard surface cleaners.
4	Amine oxide, plant derived, unspecified	Amine oxide: a biodegradable surfactant widely used in cleaning and personal care products, usually in conjunction with other surfactants. The major uses are in laundry and cleaning products, where it functions as a foam stabilizer, thickener and emollient, emulsifier, and conditioning agent.
5	Bacteria	Harmless bacteria that rapidly digest grease, proteins, and other soils. Ideal for heavy duty grease removal without solvents, and for improving slow drains.
6	Borax (see Sodium borate)	
7	Calcium chloride	A salt used to stabilize surfactant performance.
8	Carboxymethylcellulose (CMC)	A water-soluble polymer derived from natural cellulose. It helps keep soil dispersed in the wash water, thereby preventing it from re-depositing onto the fabrics being laundered. CMC is biodegraded aerobically and anaerobically by bacteria commonly found in the environment. However, its biodegradation rates range from slow to very slow.
9	Citric acid	A chelating agent (binds metals) used to replace phosphates. Citric acid is found in all living organisms and is added to processed food and beverages. It has a very favorable ecological profile due to its very low human and aquatic toxicity, and its ready biodegradability.
10	Citrus oil (see Essential oils)	Oils derived from citrus fruits such as lemons, oranges, and grapefruits.
11	Cocamide MEA	A foam stabilizer made from coconut oil. Although similar to cocamide DEA, it is less likely to form carcinogenic nitrosamines, and so is acceptable for us. Cocamide MEA is a mild eye and skin irritant. Found in: dishwashing liquids, shampoos, cosmetics.

Issue ID	Issue	Comments
12	Cocamidopropyl betaine	A surfactant derived from coconut fatty acids. It does not irritate the skin or mucous membranes. It is used to thicken shampoos, and to reduce the irritation that would result if only more irritating detergents were used.
13	Enzyme, amylase	A protein that dissolves stains caused by starchy substances.
14	Enzyme, protease	A protein that dissolves stains caused by other proteins, such as grass and blood.
15	Essential oils	A group of volatile fluids derived primarily from plants, and used in natural products primarily as fragrant additives. These components most often include a mix of alcohols, ketones, phenols, linalool, borneol, terpenes, camphor, pinene, acids, ethers, aldehydes, phenols, and sulfur, some of which may be irritating and sensitizing to the skin.
16	Ethanol (Ethyl alcohol, grain alcohol)	A volatile solvent derived from corn. Ethanol is a mild eye, skin, and respiratory tract irritant, and a central nervous system depressant. Found in: detergents, disinfectants, carpet cleaners, tub and tile cleaners, air fresheners.
17	Fir needle oil (see Essential oils)	The essential oil obtained from fir needles.
18	Fragrance, plant derived (see Essential oils)	A mixture of plant-derived essential oils added to a product to impart a scent.
19	d-Glucopyranoside	A mild surfactant derived from sugar and a fatty alcohol.
20	Grapefruit seed extract (GSE)	A natural extract that is a good source of antioxidants and allegedly provides antibacterial and anti-fungal properties. However, recent studies have confirmed that the antibacterial properties of commercially available GSE may originate from synthetic quaternary ammonium compounds (i.e. benzethonium chloride) added to the grapefruit at relatively high levels.
21	Hydrogen peroxide	A bleaching and disinfecting agent. When used for household disinfectant purposes (3% to 5%), it may be mildly irritating to the skin and mucous membranes.
22	Lactic acid	Used to adjust pH, lactic acid is made by fermentation of corn syrup.
23	Lavender oil (see Essential oils)	The essential oil obtained from lavender.
24	Lemon oil	The essential oils derived from lemon.
25	d-Limonene	A flammable, colorless liquid found in citrus oils. It has a pleasant lemon-like odor. It is used as a solvent to replace chlorinated hydro carbons and other more volatile and toxic solvents. Skin irritant, sensitizer. If ingested in sufficient quantity, may be toxic to kidneys. It is known to have natural insecticidal properties.

Issue ID	Issue	Comments
26	Magnesium chloride	A salt used to stabilize surfactant performance.
27	Methylchloroisothiazolinone/ Methylisothiazolinonea (Kathon CG)	A synthetic preservative used in cosmetics and cleaning products. At higher concentrations it is considered a sensitizer. These are not readily biodegradable at higher concentrations, but do biodegrade at very low concentrations.
28	Orange oil (see Essential oils)	The essential oils derived from oranges.
29	Quaternary amine, plant derived, unspecified	Cationic surfactants used in fabric softeners. These surfactants should not be confused with quaternary ammines used as disinfectants.
30	Salt (see Sodium chloride)	
31	Sodium borate (Borax)	A mineral composed of sodium, boron, oxygen, and water. It has detergent, fungicidal, insecticidal, preservative, and disinfectant properties. Continuous exposure to high concentrations of borax may adversely affect male fertility.
32	Sodium carbonate (soda ash, washing soda)	An alkaline salt used in detergent formulas as a water softener, that is, to remove calcium and magnesium ions from the water. Calcium and magnesium ions combine with soaps and other surfactants to form an insoluble scum that sticks to clothes and washing machine surfaces. Sodium carbonate is irritating to skin and eyes.
33	Sodium chloride (table salt)	A neutral salt often used as a filler in powders, and as a viscosity builder in liquids.
34	Sodium citrate	Sodium salt of citric acid. Sodium citrate is a chelating agent (binds metals) used to replace phosphates. Sodium citrate is found in all living organisms and is added to processed food and beverages. It has a very favorable ecological profile due to its very low human and aquatic toxicity, and its ready biodegradability.
35	Sodium gluconate	A chelating agent (binds metals). Made by the fermentation of glucose.
36	Sodium hydroxide (caustic soda, lye)	Sodium hydroxide is used to adjust the alkalinity of detergent formulas. It is derived from the electrolysis of brine (sea water) as a co-product with chlorine. It can also be mined. Concentrated solutions of sodium hydroxide are highly corrosive to the skin, and consumer products must carry a suitable warning.
37	Sodium laureth sulfate (SLES, sodium lauryl ether sulfate)	A mild, anionic surfactant used in a wide variety of home care, fabric care, and personal care products. SLES may be contaminated with 1,4-dioxane, a probable human carcinogen. However, most companies remove 1,4-dioxane contamination by a process called vacuum stripping.

Issue ID	Issue	Comments
38	Sodium laurimino-dipropionate	A surfactant derived from coconut or palm oil fatty acids.
39	Sodium percarbonate	
40	Sodium sesqui-carbonate	A chemical mixture of equal parts of soda ash and sodium bicabonate used to increase pH and total alkalinity. The pure, powdered substance is irritating to the eyes, skin and respiratory tract.
41	Sodium silicate	A salt used to provide alkalinity, soil suspension, and prevent wear of metal parts in washing machines and automatic dish washers.
42	Sodium sulfate	A salt used as a filler and to promote flow in laundry powders and automatic dishwasher powders.
43	Sorbic acid	A natural preservative used to inhibit molds, yeasts, and fungi in many foods, cosmetics, and household cleaning products. Made by the oxidation of sorbitol.
44	Sorbitol	A thickener and stabilizer. Sorbitol occurs naturally in fruits and vegetables, but most sorbitol is made from fermentation of corn syrup
45	Soy methyl esters	Soybean-derived substances used as solvents, degreasers, lubricants, and for numerous other applications.
46	Soybean oil	Oil extracted from soybeans.
47	Spruce oil (see Essential oils)	The essential oils derived from the spruce tree.
48	Surfactant, plant derived, unspecified	A plant-based surface active agent (surfactant) of unknown structure, properties, and origin.
49	Tall oil fatty acid	Fatty acids isolated from the resinous oil of trees.
50	Tea tree oil (see Essential oils)	The essential oils derived from the tea tree (melaleuca).
51	Vanilla oil (see Essential oils)	The essential oils derived from the vanilla bean.
52	Xanthan gum	A complex carbohydrate produced from bacteria (Xanthomonas campestris) fermented with a carbohydrate. It is used in food and cosmetics as a thickener, emulsifier and stabilizer. It has no known toxicity.
53	Zeolites	An inert, insoluble aluminum silicate (processed clay), that binds metals to soften water. Used as a replacement for phosphates.

Glossary

Active Ingredient. Any ingredient in a product formula that plays an active role in performing the marketed function of the product. For example, the active ingredient in many antibacterial products is triclosan, which is the chemical responsible for actually killing bacteria. The remaining ingredients assist in the delivery of this active ingredient and are sometimes called **inerts.**

Acute. The term used to describe any dramatic effects resulting from a single and often massive exposure to a product or chemical. Sudden poisonings and caustic burns are the two most common acute effects that follow certain chemical exposures.

Antibacterial. Any product or ingredient that kills bacteria in order to sanitize surfaces and materials.

Asthma. A chronic, inflammatory lung disease characterized by a narrowing of the body's airways, which results in recurrent attacks of wheezing, coughing, shortness of breath, and labored breathing.

Bioaccumulation. The process that occurs when animals and human beings repeatedly ingest a chemical over time (usually in very small doses) via air, food, and/or water, or through absorption by the skin. If the ingested chemical is persistent, it can build up, or bioaccumulate, in bodily tissues and result in a **body burden**. Bioaccumulation also refers to a specific material's slowly increasing presence in animals and people as it moves up the food chain.

Biodegradable. A term that refers to the ability of a substance or material to be broken down into its fundamental component parts by exposure to the natural action of microorganisms, sunlight, and/or water.

Body burden. A term that refers to the total amount of **persistent** chemical pollutants absorbed by the human body over time and semi-permanently stored in its tissues.

Cancer. Any of over 100 different types of disease characterized by uncontrolled cell division that results in the malignant growth of often easily-spread tumors in various bodily organs and tissues.

Caution. A regulated term used on the labels of chemical consumer products to indicate that more than one ounce must be ingested before life threatening symptoms will occur.

Chemical hypersensitivity. The condition of being sensitized to a chemical. See also **Sensitizer.**

Chlorinated compound. Any compound or chemical that contains **chlorine** atoms. Chlorinated compounds tend to exhibit the characteristics of **POPs** and, in fact, most chlorinated chemicals are classified as POPs.

Chlorine. The 11th most common element in the earth's crust, chlorine is a green-yellow gas that turns to a liquid at -34°C. It is used primarily as a disinfectant and bleaching agent, and as a raw material for a wide variety of chlorinated compounds.

Chronic. A term used to describe effects that result from repeated low-level exposures to a chemical or product over an extended period of time. Chronic health effects from exposure to chemicals include cancer and asthma.

Danger. A regulated term used on the labels of chemical consumer products to indicate that a few drops to one teaspoon of the product can be life-threatening if ingested.

Endocrine disruption. A condition where the body's endocrine (or hormonal) system is altered by exposure to certain chemicals whose molecular shape matches that of certain hormones. These chemicals are able to fit into receptors on cell surfaces that are meant for hormones, which are the body's messengers. When endocrine disruptors attach to cells they may trigger undesirable behaviors in the cell or prevent legitimate hormones from attaching and delivering their signals.

EPA. The Environmental Protection Agency, the federal agency charged with ensuring a clean, safe, and healthy environment.

General biocide. An **antibacterial** chemical capable of disrupting so many different cellular functions at once that bacteria encountering it cannot survive. General biocide antibacterial products do not contribute to the rising problem of disinfectant- and antibiotic-resistant "super bug" bacteria. See also **specific biocide.**

Greenwashing. A spin on the term "whitewashing," greenwashing occurs when manufacturers attempt to label a product "green" or "environmentally friendly" when in fact there's little or no difference between the product in question and regular products of its kind.

Hormonal disruption. See Endocrine disruption

Hydrocarbon. Any compound consisting only of hydrogen and carbon atoms. Petroleum consists of many different hydrocarbon compounds connected together on a "chain." Breaking this chain apart separates these various hydrocarbon compounds for use as the basis of synthetic chemicals.

Inerts. The catch-all name for ingredients that are not considered **active ingredients.** Inert ingredients have no role in performing the actual marketed function of the product but are added as buffering agents, solvents, preservatives, dispersal agents and carriers, wetting agents, fillers, and other ingredients that help stabilize, dispense, and increase the potency, effectiveness, and ease-of-use of the product. Inerts are frequently more toxic than active ingredients.

Lethal dose (LD). A scientific standard used to measure the potential of a given substance to cause death in humans. Lethal Dose standards use a benchmark known as LD50, or the amount of a compound in milligrams per kilogram of body weight needed to cause death in 50 percent of test animals exposed to this quantity.

Material Safety Data Sheets (MSDS). A standardized chemical information summary sheet that provides varying degrees of information about the chemicals, products, or formulas used by a specific facility or in a specific product. The use of MSDSs in manufacturing and commercial settings is required by the Occupational Safety and Health Administration.

Multiple chemical sensitivities (MCS). Also known as environmental illness, MCS is believed to be an acquired allergic disease. It is characterized by a wide variety of potential symptoms that affect any number of bodily organs or systems and that appear when the victim is exposed to trigger chemicals in tiny or even trace amounts.

National Toxicology Program. A program of the Department of Health and Human Services created in 1978 to coordinate toxicology testing programs within the federal government, strengthen the science base in toxicology, develop and validate improved testing methods, and provide information about potentially toxic chemicals to health, regulatory, and research agencies, scientific and medical communities, and the public.

Off-gassing. See **out-gassing.**

Optical brightener. One of a number of chemicals primarily added to laundry detergents to make fabrics seem brighter or whiter. Optical brighteners coat clothes and other materials with fluorescent particles that convert ultraviolet light into visible light and reflect it outward to make the object appear cleaner than it actually is.

Out-gassing. The process by which the chemical compounds contained in synthetic materials break down over time and are slowly released into the air in the form of toxic fumes.

Persistent. A term used to describe compounds able to resist the natural forces of decomposition and remain intact in the environment once released. Persistent chemicals are not readily **biodegradable** and instead maintain their ability to cause harm long after their manufacture and use.

Persistent organic pollutants (POPs). A new category of existing chemicals that attempts to classify synthetic substances not by their molecular composition but by their behavior in the environment. To earn this classification, a substance must resist decomposition, tend to accumulate in body fat, be able to travel great distances in the environment, and be linked to serious hormonal, reproductive, neurological, and immune disorders.

Petrochemical. Any synthetic compound composed in some part of hydrocarbons obtained from petroleum.

Poison. See **Danger.**

Potentiation. The process by which interactions between the chemicals found in different products enhance the potential for harm of some or all of the individual chemicals involved.

Precautionary Principle. An important new environmental philosophy and regulatory framework in which places the burden of proof for the safety of an activity or product on its proponents rather than its opponents. Until this safety can be proven, the Precautionary Principle states that safety measures should be taken even if direct evidence that the activity or product may cause harm is lacking and only suspicions exist. The precautionary measures that should be considered include halting the activity or product until its non-hazardous nature can be confirmed.

Sensitizer. Any chemical that causes a substantial proportion of people to develop an allergic response to it after repeated exposures. See also **chemical hypersensitivity.**

Solvent. Any of a large group of easily evaporated chemicals used to dissolve or disperse other materials, especially oils. Often called degreasers, solvents are also used in consumer products to keep other ingredients suspended and dispersed in the product.

Specific biocide. An **antibacterial** chemical that kills bacteria by targeting and interfering with very specific cellular functions. Because specific biocides mimic the strategies of antibiotics, bacteria can evolve in their presence and become resistant to them. See also **general biocide.**

Surfactant. A synthetic detergent that performs the functions traditionally handled by old-fashioned soap. Surfactants are molecules with two ends that form a "bridge" between the grease and dirt being cleaned and the water doing the work. This linking action allows the former to dissolve into the latter.

Synthesis. The process that occurs when the substances in different products accidentally or intentionally come into contact with each other and chemically combine to create brand new unanticipated compounds.

Volatile organic compounds (VOCs). Carbon-based chemicals that can form vapors at room temperature. Like **solvents** (most of which can also be classified as VOCs), they are easily evaporated into our homes' air and come from two predominant sources: the release of toxic gases from synthetic materials like foams and plastics and the use of toxic cleaning products and other household chemicals.

Warning. A regulated term used on the labels of chemical consumer products to indicate that one teaspoon to one ounce of the product can be life threatening if ingested.

Resource Guide

As you've no doubt noticed by now, our book concerns some pretty big subjects. In fact, the issues we've written about are too big for just one book to cover completely. The good news is that we don't have to do it all. Instead, our book can focus on providing an overview of the many issues at hand because a wide variety of excellent resources already supply all the secondary information and scientific details that would otherwise make this book too heavy to lift, let alone read!

We think of our book as a kind of "Introduction to Household Chemicals and Home Cleaning 101." When you're ready to learn more, which you are now that you've made it here, this section provides a reading list for your continuing education. It represents a more advanced course on the subject that we urge each of our readers to take.

The following resources represent the very best we've found in our 17-year quest to help consumers create healthier homes and live safer lives. In compiling this list, we've done our very best to make sure the websites we recommend are still active and that the books we suggest are all still available. In both the Internet and publishing worlds, however, things often change rapidly. A website that's online today may vanish into the digital ether by nightfall. A book that's in print this afternoon may not be by this time tomorrow. While there's unfortunately nothing we can do about disappearing websites, if you find that any books we recommend have become unavailable, we suggest checking with your local library or used book dealers for a copy. Similarly, online resources like the used book market Alibris.com and the auction site E-bay.com are excellent places to search out titles that are no longer in print. In these cases, we promise that the effort will be well worth it.

One last note: we've listed our resources in priority order. While all the books and web sites listed here have much of value to offer, those at the top of their respective categories are our number one choices. If your time or interest is limited, starting at the beginning of these categories and exploring those resources we list first will yield the greatest informational dividends.

The Non-Toxic Times

Though it may seem a bit egocentric to say it, we're not shy, and we also believe that it's true: one of the best resources on the Internet is our own free publication, *The Non-Toxic Times*. The official e-newsletter of Seventh Generation, it covers a wide variety of topics relating to toxics in the home and environment. Delivered via e-mail, each monthly edition offers a wealth of current news and views, strategies for healthier living, information on specific hazards and safer alternatives, book and website reviews, and other related features. To sign up for a free subscription, go to <www.seventhgeneration.com>.

Scientific and Advocacy Resources

The following websites and books are recommended for further information about the science of toxic chemicals, their regulation by government agencies, and the political issues involved.

Our Stolen Future, Theo Colburn, Dianne Dumanoski, and John Peterson Myers, Plume/Penguin, 1997. If you only read one book on this list, this is the one we recommend. It explains how chlorine, dioxins and other hazardous toxins cause reproductive, developmental, endocrine, and immune system disorders. A continually updated companion website follows the latest developments in the areas the book addresses.
Website: www.ourstolenfuture.org

Toxic Deception: How the Chemical Industry Manipulates Science, Bends the Law, and Endangers Your Health, Dan Fagin, Marianne Lavelle, and the Center for Science in the Public Interest, Birch Lane Press, 1996. An exceptional book that explains in great detail why governments are not protecting us from dangerous chemicals.

Living Downstream: An Ecologist Looks at Cancer and the Environment, Sandra Steingraber, Addison Wesley, 1997. Well-researched and beautifully written, this book compellingly documents the author's case that 80 percent of all cancer is environmentally related and carefully looks at the chemicals that may be to blame.

Environmental Health News offers a comprehensive website and a free daily e-mail news service that track current news stories and magazine articles concerning toxics and related issues.
Website: www.environmentalhealthnews.org

The Environmental Working Group provides background information and current study results on the issue of body burdens.
Website: www.bodyburden.org

It also maintains an excellent toxics-focused website that provides current news, background information, study results, and opportunities for participation in advocacy campaigns.
Website: www.ewg.org

Rachel's Environment and Health Weekly is an outstanding e-newsletter published periodically by the Environmental Research Foundation.
Website: www.rachel.org/bulletin

Trust Us, We're Experts, Sheldon Rampton and John Stauber, Jeremy Tarcher/Putnam, 2001. An eye-opening book that exposes the ways in which industries and corporations use public relations and other forms of spin to manipulate science and public opinion in ways favorable to their bottom lines but unfavorable to human health.

Pandora's Poison, Joe Thornton, MIT Press, 2000. The benchmark reference work about the extreme environmental and public health dangers of chlorine and chlorinated chemicals like dioxins.

Generations at Risk, Ted Schettler, Gina Solomon, et. al., MIT Press, 1999. This volume examines the evidence that exposure to chemical toxins is affecting human reproduction and development.

Toxics A - Z: A Guide to Everyday Pollution Hazards, John Harte, Cheryl Holdren, Richard Schneider, and Christine Shirley, University of California Press, 1991. A pollutant-by-pollutant look at the key players in the chemical contamination of both the environment and human beings.

Staying Well in a Toxic World, Lynn Lawson, The Noble Press, 1993. One of the first books to address issues like multiple chemical sensitivities and sick building syndrome, this volume retains its currency today.

Our Toxic World, A Wake Up Call, Dr. Doris Rapp, Environmental Medical Research Foundation, 2004. This fact-packed volume looks at the ways in which our world has become contaminated by chemicals and technologies and integrates a wide range of evidence with advice from an expert on what you can do to stay healthier.

The Center for Health, Environment and Justice maintains a website with a healthy mix of toxins information, advocacy and activism. Website: www.chej.org

Chem-tox.com maintains an ongoing overview of the latest research findings on health disorders linked to exposure to common chemicals and pesticides.
Website: www.chem-tox.com

Healthy Home and Cleaning Resources

The following resources are filled with information concerning toxins found in common consumer products, safer alternatives, strategies for healthier living, and other related ideas.

Creating a Healthy Household: The Ultimate Guide for Healthier, Safer, Less-Toxic Living, Lynn Marie Bower, Healthy House Institute, 2000. This volume is perhaps the last word in healthy home books. Clocking in at just over 700 pages, it's the ultimate compendium on all matters of non-toxic living.

Better Basics for the Home, Annie Berthold Bond, Three Rivers Press, 1999. A highly recommended book filled with creative and effective do-it-yourself recipes for homemade cleaners, personal care products, pet supplies, garden needs, house care items, and more.

Home Safe Home: Protecting Yourself and Your Family from Everyday Toxics and Harmful Household Products, Debra Lynn Dadd, Jeremy P. Tarcher/Putnam, 1997. One of the best books of its kind and a seminal reference in the healthy home field, there are few related topics this volume doesn't touch upon.

Safe Shopper's Bible: A Consumer's Guide to Non-Toxic Household Products, Cosmetics, and Food, David Steinman and Samuel S. Epstein, M.D., Macmillan, 1995. This book has the most complete evaluation of brand name household products we've ever seen. Highly recommended.

A Consumer's Dictionary of Household, Yard and Office Chemicals, Ruth Winter, Crown Publishing, 1992. Though out of print, this dictionary is well worth seeking out for the quick and easy work it makes of demystifying the often incomprehensible ingredients panels on household products. If you ever wondered what those unpronounceable ingredients are, this book will tell you.

Homes That Heal, Athena Thompson, New Society Publishers, 2004. The most recent entry in the healthy home category, this book is extremely comprehensive and benefits further from being written in an accessible and engaging style.

The Green Guide is a bi-monthly magazine devoted to healthier and more environmentally sustainable non-toxic living, available in both paper and electronic versions. Filled with tips, advice, information, and answers, it's an essential publication.
Website: www.thegreenguide.com

The Cancer Prevention Coalition maintains an excellent informational website covering cancer from a preventative healthy living perspective.
Website: www.preventcancer.com

Living Healthy in a Toxic World, David Steinman and R. Michael Wisner, Perigee, 1996. A good introduction to the art of safer living, but by no means the most exhaustive one.

Online Toxics Databases

These online resources will guide you to detailed information concerning the potential health hazards and safe handling of specific products and chemical ingredients.

MSDS Search.com connects you to over three dozen online repositories of MSDSs. Search by chemical name, manufacturer, or product. Also offers a rich variety of MSDS-related information and services.
Website: www.msdssearch.com

The Household Products database of the National Institutes of Health is a one-stop shop for information about the potential chemical hazards hiding in over 5,000 consumer products.
Website: http://hpd.nlm.nih.gov

Extoxnet is a source of objective, science-based information about pesticides and other toxins written for laypeople. Includes a searchable database of pesticide safety data.
Website: http://extoxnet.orst.edu

Children's Issues

These resources are focused on toxics issues as they relate to children.

Raising Healthy Children in a Toxic World, 101 Smart Solutions for Every Family, Philip Landrigan and Herbert Needleman, Rodale Press, 2002. An important volume every parent should read, this book covers everything from household cleaners and electromagnetic fields to pesticides and synthetic hormones. It's a vital reference tool that succeeds in its goal of helping to create a safer world for children both at home and away.

The Center for Children's Health and the Environment is the nation's first academic research and policy center to examine the links between exposure to toxic pollutants and childhood illness. Website: www.childenvironment.org

Healthy Child Online is a resource from the Future Generations partnership, which is dedicated to protecting children by disseminating information on healthier child-rearing strategies, and unhealthy children's products and other hazards. Website: www.healthychild.com

The Children's Health and Environmental Coalition (CHEC) is an excellent introductory resource, especially for those with children. Their HealtheHouse is a nicely interactive virtual tour of a typical house that highlights common trouble spots. First Steps is special monthly e-mail service for expectant parents, those with infants, or those with toddlers. Website: www.checnet.org

Healthy Homes, Healthy Kids, Joyce M. Schoemaker and Charity Y. Vitale, Island Press, 1991. A good overview of some of the many steps that parents can take to protect their children from common household hazards.

Healthy Indoor Air

Many of the resources in the Healthy Home and Cleaning Resources section contain information on indoor air pollution issues and solutions. Here are some that deal solely with this subject.

House Dangerous: Indoor Air Pollution in Your Home and Office and What You Can Do About It, Ellen Greenfield, Interlink Books, 1991. This book offers a good overview of the issue of indoor air quality as well as advice on identifying and solving problems.

How to Grow Fresh Air: 50 Houseplants the Purify Your Home and Office, B.C. Wolverton, Penguin Books, 1996. This useful reference identifies those houseplants that have proved particularly adept at removing toxins from indoor air. Profiles of each plant are supplemented by several chapters of background that explain how plants clean air and how consumers can harness this ability.

The American Lung Association maintains information about indoor air pollution. Website: www.lungusa.org

Multiple Chemical Sensitivities/ Environmental Illness

These resources are dedicated to collecting and disseminating current information on MCS, an often misunderstood and misdiagnosed condition.

An informative website created by an MCS sufferer, MCS Survivors.com is filled with invaluable resources and is engaged in an ongoing effort to organize the growing body of web-based MCS information and resources.
Website: www.mcsurvivors.com

The Environmental Illness Society of Canada is a professional organization offering conferences, resources, and other help to victims of this condition.
Website: www.eisc.ca/index1.html

The Chemical Injury Information Network provides much-needed help with the medical and legal problems that so often accompany the onset of MCS.
Website: www.ciin.org

MCS Referral & Resources offers professional outreach, patient support, and public advocacy devoted to the diagnosis, treatment, accommodation, and prevention of MCS.
Website: www.mcsrr.org

The Health and Environment Resource Center maintains informational resources, news articles, and message boards focused on environmental illness.
Website: www.herc.org

Living Without is a quarterly magazine that offers a guide to living with all manner of sensitivities to everything from foods to chemicals. Discussions cover a wide variety of health issues including allergies, food sensitivities and intolerances, multiple chemical sensitivities, eating disorders, asthma, diabetes, dermatitis, gastroenterology-related disorders and others.
Website: www.livingwithout.com

Notes

Introduction

1. Sandra Steingraber, *Living Downstream,* Addison-Wesley, 1997, page 131.

2. The Carcinogenicity Potency Project, Carcinogenicity Potency Database, [online], [cited July 11, 2005], May 17, 2005, http://potency.berkeley.edu/cpdb.html

3. Steingraber, *Living Downstream,* page 61.

4. D.A. Sterling, Presentation at National Center for Health Statistics Conference, Washington, DC, July 15, 1991; "Further Investigation of Housewife Cancer Mortality Risk," *Women and Health,* 1982, 7:43-51; W.E. Morton and T.J Unga, "Cancer Mortality in the Major Cottage Industry," *Women and Health,* 1979, 4:346-354; M.N. Gleason, R.E. Gosselin, H.C. Hodge, and R.P. Smith, *Clinical Toxicology of Commercial Products,* Williams and Wilkins, 1969.

5. Peter Montague, "Human Breast Milk Is Contaminated," *Rachel's Environment and Health News,* No. 193, August 8, 1990.

6. Steingraber, *Living Downstream,* page 239.

7. The National Environmental Trust, "Cabinet Confidential," July, 2004.

8. Ibid.

9. Douglas Fischer, "The Body Chemical," *The Oakland Tribune,* March 8, 2005.

10. Ibid.

11. The Asthma and Allergy Foundation of America, *Allergy Facts and Figures,* [online], [cited February 21, 2005], www.aafa.org/display.cfm?id=9&sub=30

12. Peter Montague, "A New Mechanism of Disease?" *Rachel's Environment and Health Weekly,* No. 585, February 12, 1998.

Chapter 2: Our Homes as Test Tubes

1. Steve Waygood, "Uncertainty Persists on Chemical Equations," *Environmental Finance,* September 2004.
2. Jane Kay, "Home is Where the Hazard Is," *San Francisco Chronicle,* May 19, 2004.
3. Rochelle Smith, "Green Cleaners: Great for Your Customers and the Environment," *Natural Foods Merchandiser,* March 1995, page 132.
4. Children's Health Environmental Coalition, *Not Under My Roof,* [online], [cited February 2005], www.checnet.org/ prodres_myroof.asp
5. Steve Waygood, "Uncertainty Persists on Chemical Equations," *Environmental Finance,* September 2004.
6. Michael P. Wilson and James E. Cone, "REACHing for Chemical Safety," *San Francisco Chronicle,* October 21, 2003.
7. "Alarm Bells Silent on Teflon," *The Daily News & Independent Online,* November 25, 2004, www.dailynews.co.za/index. php?fSectionId=541&fArticleId=2313155

Chapter 3: Household Chemicals and Cancer

1. Cancer Prevention Coalition, "The Stop Cancer Before It Starts Campaign, How to Win the Losing War on Cancer," February 2003.
2. Ibid.
3. Ibid.
4. Sandra Steingraber, *Living Downstream,* Addison-Wesley, 1997, page 59.
5. Ibid., page 59.
6. Ibid., page 60.
7. Ibid., page 131.
8. D.A. Sterling, Presentation at National Center for Health Statistics Conference, Washington, DC, July 15, 1991; W.E. Morton, "Further Investigation of Housewife Cancer Mortality Risk," *Women and Health,* 1982, 7:43-51; W.E. Morton, and T.J Unga, "Cancer Mortality in the Major Cottage Industry," *Women and Health,* 1979, 4:346-354; M.N. Gleason, R.E. Gosselin, H.C. Hodge, and R.P. Smith, "Clinical Toxicology of Commercial Products," Williams and Wilkins, 1969.
9. Jane E. Brody, "Another Source of Air Pollution: The Home," *The New York Times,* January 16, 2001.

Chapter 4: Household Chemicals and Asthma

1. American Public Health Association and Harvard Medical School press release, "Experts: Childhood Asthma 'Epidemic' Among Inner-City Youths Seen in Absence of Steps to Curb Global Warming, Fossil Fuel Use," April 29, 2004.
2. President's Task Force on Environmental Health Risks and Safety Risks to Children, "Asthma and the Environment: A Strategy to Protect Children," May 2000.

3. Selena Ricks, "Understanding Asthma." *Portland Press Herald,* March 21, 2004.

4. American Public Health Association and Harvard Medical School press release, "Experts: Childhood Asthma 'Epidemic' Among Inner-City Youths Seen in Absence of Steps to Curb Global Warming, Fossil Fuel Use," April 29, 2004.

5. Ibid.

6. Figure derived by subtracting figure in footnote 11 from total national asthma costs cited in footnote 9, Chapter 3.

7. K. Rumchev et. al., "Association of Domestic Exposure to Volatile Organic Compounds With Asthma in Young Children," *Thorax,* 2004, 59: 746 -751.

8. M. Medina-Ramon et. al., "Asthma Symptoms In Women Employed in Domestic Cleaning," *Thorax,* 2003, 58:950-4.

9. K.D. Rosenman et. al., "Cleaning Products and Work-Related Asthma," *Journal of Occupational Environmental Medicine,* May 2003, 45:556-63.

10. Peter Montague, "Asthma: Prevention May be the Only Cure," *Rachel's Environment and Health News,* No. 374, January 27, 1994.

11. A. Karjalainen, R. Martikainen, J. Karjalainen, T. Klaukka, and K. Kurppa, "Excess Incidence of Asthma Among Finnish Cleaners Employed In Different Industries, *European Respiratory Journal,* January 2002, 19: 90-95.

12. M.T. Salam, Y.F. Li, B. Langholz, and F.D. Gilliland, "Early Life Environmental Risk Factors for Asthma: Findings from the Children's Health Study," [online], [cited May 2005], *Environmental Health Perspectives,* Volume 112, Number 6, May 2004,

    http://ehp.niehs.nih.gov/members/2003/6662/6662.html

Chapter 5: Household Chemicals and Hormonal Disruption

1. Marla Cone, "River Pollution Study Finds Hormonal Defects in Fish," *Los Angeles Times,* September 22, 1998.

2. Theo Colburn, Dianne Dumanoski, and John Peterson Myers, *Our Stolen Future,* Plume/Penguin, 1997, page 129.

3. Our Stolen Future.org, "Widespread Pollutants with Endocrine-disrupting Effects," [online], [cited November 2004], www.ourstolenfuture.org/Basics/chemlist.htm

4. N. Akhtar, S.A. Kayani, M.M. Ahmad, and M. Shahab, "Insecticide-induced changes in secretory activity of the thyroid gland in rats," *Journal of Applied Toxicology,* 1996, 16(5):397-400.

5. L. Kembra et. al., "Exposure to Bisphenol-A Advances Puberty," *Nature,* No. 401, October 21, 1999, pages 763-764.

6. "Environmental Estrogen Shown To Affect Sperm," Reuters News Service, July 3, 2002.

Chapter 6: Household Chemicals and Multiple Chemical Sensitivities

1. Peter Montague, "A New Mechanism of Disease?" *Rachel's Environment and Health Weekly,* No.

585, February 12, 1998.

2. Ibid.

Chapter 7: The Burden Our Bodies Bear

1. US Environmental Protection Agency Office of Toxic Substances, "Analysis of Human Adipose Tissue, Volume 1: Technical Approach," [online], [cited May 2005], 1987, www.chemicalbodyburden. org/whatisbb.htm

2. Department of Health and Human Services, Centers for Disease Control, "Second National Report on Human Exposure to Environmental Chemicals" [online], [cited May 2005], January, 2003, www.cdc.gov/exposurereport/

3. The Environmental Working Group, "Body Burden: The Pollution in People. Executive Summary: What We Found," [online], [cited October 2004], www.ewg.org/reports/bodyburden/es.php

Chapter 11: Bad Behavior

1. Biodegradable plastics have reappeared again in the last few years. This new generation of plastics is based on a technology that uses vegetable-based products like corn to create a natural polymer called PLA, a theoretically biodegradable plastic. While the decomposition of PLA is largely only successful when it's carefully composted (a fact which makes any broad claim of biodegradability dubious at best), these new materials offer an important benefit in sustainability because they are made from renewable raw materials instead of non-renewable petroleum. Even though the source of these renewable materials is currently genetically modified corn (a technology with many risks and a suspect safety record), the technology behind them offers much hope and is worthy of consideration.

2. "Alarm Bells Silent on Teflon," *The Daily News & Independent Online,* [online], [cited May 2005], November 25, 2004, www.dailynews.co.za/index.php?fSectionId=541&fArticleId=2313155

3. Douglas Fischer, "The Body Chemical," *The Oakland Tribune,* March 8, 2005.

4. Ruth Winter, *A Consumers Dictionary of Household, Yard and Office Chemicals,* Crown Publishers, 1992, page 20.

5. Ian Sample, "Chemical Cocktails Make a Potent Mix," *New Scientist,* March 30, 2002.

Chapter 12: Acute vs. Chronic

1. William A. Watson et. al., "2003 Annual Report of the American Association of Poison Control Centers Toxic Exposure Surveillance System," *American Journal of Emergency Medicine,* Vol. 22, No. 5, September 2004.

Chapter 13: What Dose Makes the Poison?

1. William A. Watson et. al., "2003 Annual Report of the American Association of Poison Control Centers Toxic Exposure Surveillance System." *American Journal of Emergency Medicine,* Vol. 22, No. 5, September 2004.

2. "Peanut Allergies a Growing Problem," Reuters News Service, [online], [Cited May 2005], December 9, 2003, www.msnbc.msn.com/id/3671615/

Chapter 14: A Quick Look at Material Safety Data Sheets

1. This definition contains two parts: Health Hazard and Physical Hazard. A health hazard means a chemical for which there is statistically significant evidence based on at least one study conducted in accordance with established scientific principles that acute or chronic health effects may occur in exposed employees. A physical hazard means a chemical for which there is scientifically valid evidence that it is a combustible liquid, a compressed gas, explosive, flammable, an organic peroxide, an oxidizer, pyrophoric, unstable (reactive), or water-reactive.

2. Interactive Learning Paradigms, "Frequently Asked Questions About Materials Safety Data Sheets," [online], [cited October 2004], 1995, www.ilpi.com/msds/faq/index.html

3. Ted Schettler MD MPH, Gina Solomon MD, Maria Valenti, Annette Huddle, *Generations at Risk,* MIT Press, 1999, pages 259-260, 289-290; Debra Lynn Dadd, *Home Safe Home,* Tarcher/ Putnam, 1997, page 21; David Steinman and Samuel S. Epstein, *The Safe Shopper's Bible,* Macmillan, 1995, pages 10 and 18.

Chapter 15: Household Chemicals and the World Outside

1. All figures: Gary Polakovic, "Chemicals in Home a Big Smog Source," *Los Angeles Times,* March 9, 2003.

2. Rochelle Smith, "Green Cleaners: Great for Your Customers and the Environment," *Natural Foods Merchandiser,* March 1995, Page 132.

3. Lono Kahuna Kupua A'o, *Don't Drink the Water,* Kali Press, 1996, page 15.

4. James Politte, *What's In The Water,* [online], [cited October 2004], *Environmental Science and Technology,* July 22, 2002, www.chemistry.org/portal/a/c/s/1/feature_ent.html?id=6b3d4d8c3ff711d6ea384fd8fe800100

5. All hydrocarbon chemicals are known as organic chemicals. But don't let the name fool you! Unlike organic foods or organic lawn care products, organic chemicals aren't necessarily 100 percent natural. They get their "organic" label because they're based on carbon, the molecular foundation of life, not because they consist of harmless compounds that naturally occur in the environment. Quite the contrary, countless so-called "organic" chemicals are some of the most synthetic things ever created by human beings!

6. Distributed Active Archive Center, NASA, *Pollution at Sea,* [online], [cited February 2005], http://daac.gsfc.nasa.gov/CAMPAIGN_DOCS/OCDST/shuttle_oceanography_web/oss_ 122.html; SeaWiFS Project, NASA Goddard Space Flight Center, *Threats to the Health of Oceans,* [online], [cited February 2005], http://seawifs.gsfc.nasa.gov/OCEAN_PLANET/ HTML/education_threats.html

7. Sustainable Energy and Economic Development, *Bush Energy Plan is Dirty, Dangerous and Doesn't Deliver for Consumers,* [online], [cited May 2005], May 16, 2001, www.seedcoalition.org/pc010516.htm

Part Three: The Dirty Secrets of Household Cleaners

1. Euromonitor International, *Household Cleaning Products in U.S.,* July, 2002.

Chapter 16: The Incredible Case of the Shrinking Label

1. The National Environmental Trust, *Cabinet Confidential,* July, 2004.

2. Debra Lynn Dadd, *Home Safe Home,* Tarcher/Putnam, 1997, page 74.

Chapter 17: Test- and Approval-Free for You and Me

1. Federal jurisdiction over modern chemicals takes the form of a confusing hodgepodge of regulations and responsibility scattered over several agencies. In general, the EPA is responsible for initially approving a chemical for manufacture and use in what is largely a rubber stamp process. Once placed inside a consumer product like a household cleaner, that chemical and its host formula become the province of the Consumer Product Safety Commission, which lacks authority to prevent a product's initial introduction and can't restrict or ban a product from being sold until and unless it can demonstrate that that product represents a significant risk and that the benefits of regulating it would be greater than the costs. If the chemical is intended for use in cosmetics or personal care products, the FDA has authority, but this agency also requires no review of chemical ingredients and can only act after the fact.

2. Ruth Winter, *A Consumers Dictionary of Household, Yard and Office Chemicals,* Crown Publishers, 1992, page 9; Dan Fagin, Marianne Lavelle, Center for Public Integrity, *Toxic Deception,* Birch Lane Press, 1996, page 219 ff.

3. Coming Clean.org., *Reason #1 to Join Coming Clean,* [online], [cited September 2004], January 2001, www.come-clean. org/reason_1.htm

4. Debra Lynn Dadd, *Home Safe Home,* Tarcher/Putnam, 1997, page 73.

Chapter 18: Meet the Usual Suspects

1. Ruth Winter, *A Consumers Dictionary of Household, Yard and Office Chemicals,* Crown Publishers, 1992, page 99.

2. Kim Erickson, *Drop Dead Gorgeous,* Contemporary Books, 2002, Page 24.

3. Lynn Marie Bower, *The Healthy Household,* Healthy House Institute, 1995, page 47.

4. David Steinman and Samuel S. Epstein, *The Safe Shopper's Bible,* Macmillan, 1995, pages 72-73.

5. *Fast Company,* "Gunter Pauli Cleans Up, A Fast Company Conversation," [online], [cited October 2004], November, 1993, www.fastcompany.com/online/00/pauli.html

6. David Steinman and R. Michael Wisner, *Living Healthy in a Toxic World,* Perigee Books, 1996, page 13.

7. The National Environmental Trust, *Cabinet Confidential,* July, 2004.

8. Cate Jenkins, EPA Office Of Solid Waste And Emergency Response, "Criminal Investigation of Monsanto Corporation — Cover-up of Dioxin Contamination in Products — Falsification of Dioxin Health Studies," [online], [cited May 2005], November 15, 1990, www.ibiblio.org/ pub/academic/history/ marshall/military/vietnam/nvet_archive/nvet0501.txt

Chapter 19: Unpronounceably Unhealthy

1. Chart compiled from the following sources:

Ruth Winter, *A Consumers Dictionary of Household, Yard and Office Chemicals*, Crown Publishers, 1992.

Annie Berthold-Bond, *Clean and Green*, Ceres Press, 1994.

Martin Wolf et. al., *Understanding the Chemicals Used in Common Household Cleaners*, Seventh Generation, 1998.

Debra Lynn Dadd, *Home Safe Home*, Jeremy P. Tarcher, 1997.

Annie Berthold-Bond, *Better Basics for the Home*, Three Rivers Press, 1999.

Chapter 20: Germ Warfare and Human Welfare

1. CBC News, *Exposure to Dust May Protect Against Allergies*, [online], [cited May 2005], September 19, 2002, www.cbc.ca/stories/2002/09/18/ dust020918

2. National Jewish Medical and Research Center News, *Bacterial Infections Alter Allergic Response*, [online], [cited May 2005], February 25, 2003, www.nationaljewish.org/diseaseinfo/ diseases/allergy/about/causes/bacterial.aspx

3. Zerah Lurie, "In a Lather Over Antibacterial Products, More and More Products Tout This Benefit, but There is Little Actual Science Behind It," *Newsday*, July 20, 2004, page B48.

4. Ibid.

5. Rebecca Renner, "From Triclosan to Dioxin," *Environmental Science and Technology*, June 1, 2002.

6. James Politte, "What's In The Water," [online], [cited October 2004], *Environmental Sceience and Technology*, July 22, 2002.

7. Environmental Defense Fund. *Scorecard: The Pollution Information Site*, [online], [cited August 2004], www.scorecard.org/chemicalprofiles/hazard-detail.tcl?edf_substance_id=3380%2d34%2d5 &short_list_name=wmp%5feco

Chapter 26: Coming Clean in the Kitchen, Part Two

1. Many people believe that phosphates were banned from household cleaning products in the 1970s. While this is largely true, the automatic dishwasher detergent industry was able to obtain an exemption. As a result, most dishwasher detergents still contain this ingredient and remain a serious threat to ponds and small lakes.

Chapter 27: Perfluorochemicals

1. Environmental Working Group, "PFCs: A Family of Chemicals That Contaminate the Planet," [online], [cited October 2005], hwww.ewg.org/reports/pfcworld/

2. Environmental Working Group, "EWG PFCs Issue Page," [online], [cited October 2005], www.ewg.org/issues/pfcs/index.php

3. World Wildlife Fund, "Stockholm Convention: 'New POPs' — Screening Additional POPs Candidates," April, 2005.

4. Environmental Working Group, "PFCs: A Family of Chemicals That Contaminate the Planet," [online], [cited October 2005], www.ewg.org/reports/pfcworld/

5. Environmental Protection Agency, "Perfluorooctanoic Acid Risk Assessment (PFOA) Draft Report for Review at the July 6, 2005 Public Teleconference," [online], [cited October 2005], www.epa.gov/sab/pdf/rev_draft_pfoa_ex_sum-report_w-intro_062705.pdf

6. Environmental Working Group, "PFCs: A Family of Chemicals That Contaminate the Planet," [online], [cited October 2005], www.ewg.org/reports/pfcworld/

7. World Wildlife Fund, "Stockholm Convention: 'New POPs' — Screening Additional POPs Candidates," April, 2005.

8. Environmental Working Group, "PFCs: A Family of Chemicals That Contaminate the Planet," [online], [cited October 2005], www.ewg.org/reports/pfcworld/

Chapter 29: Devils in the Dust

1. Cornell University Ergonomics Web, Lecture DEA350, "Ambient Environment: Ventilation Basics," [online], [cited August 2004],

   http://ergo.human.cornell.edu/studentdownloads/ DEA350notes/Vent/ventnotes.html

2. Doris Black, "Healthy Home Improvement," *Santa Cruz Sentinel Home & Garden Supplement,* Spring, 2003.

3. Hannah Holmes, *The Secret Life of Dust,* John Wiley & Sons, 2001, page 7.

4. Clean Production Action, *Sick of Dust,* March, 2005.

5. American College of Asthma, Allergy, and Immunology, "Advice From Your Allergist — House Dust Allergy," [online], [cited August 2004], www.acaai.org/public/advice/dust.htm

Chapter 33: Airing Our Dirty Laundry

1. "Fun Laundry Facts," *Hanging Out,* the Project Laundry List Newsletter, July, 2000.

Chapter 35: Why Our Littlest Ones Face the Largest Risk
From Our Homes' Biggest Hazards

1. The National Environmental Trust, *Cabinet Confidential,* July, 2004.

2. Philip J.Landrigan, and Joy E. Carlson, "Environmental Policy and Children's Health," [online], [cited May 2005], The Future of Children, Fall 1995, www.futureofchildren. org/usr_doc/vol5no2ART4.pdf

3. Philip Landrigan, "A Doctor's Viewpoint: Why Air Pollutants Harm Kids," [online], [cited December, 2005], Children's Health Environmental Coalition, September 2003, www.checnet. org/healthehouse/education/ articles-detail.asp?Main_ID=659

4. Joyce Schoemaker and Charity Vitale, *Healthy Homes, Healthy Kids,* Island Press, 1991, page 4.

5. Philip J. Landrigan and Joy E. Carlson, "Environmental Policy and Children's Health," The Future of Children, Fall, 1995, www.futureofchildren.org/usr_doc/vol5no2ART4.pdf

6. Philip J. Landrigan et. al., "Environmental Pollutants and Disease In American Children: Estimates Of Morbidity, Mortality And Costs For Lead Poisoning, Asthma, Cancer And Developmental Disabilities," [online], [cited December, 2005], Center for Children's Health and the Environment, www.childenvironment.org/reports/Environmental-PAPER.htm

7. "Cleaning Products Wheezing Link," [online], [cited December 2004], BBC News, December 23, 2004, news.bbc.co.uk/2/hi/health/4115617.stm

Chapter 36: A Baker's Dozen Ways to Help Kids Breathe Easier

1. The National Environmental Trust, *Cabinet Confidential,* July, 2004.

Chapter 37: Just Say No to VOCs

1. Aerosols Harm Mother and Baby, [online], [cited December, 2004], BBC News, October, 19, 2004, news.bbc.co.uk/go/pr/fr/-/1/hi/health/ 3752188.stm

2. K. Rumchev et. al., "Association of Domestic Exposure to Volatile Organic Compounds With Asthma in Young Children," *Thorax,* 2004, 59:746 -751.

Chapter 38: Phthalates Are No Phun

1. *Plastics Components Linked to Allergies in Kids,* [online], [cited December, 2004], Reuters News Service, October 8, 2004, www.planetark.com/dailynewsstory.cfm?newsid=27588

Part Six: Breathing Easier Indoors

1. Michael C. Mix et. al., *Biology: Network of Life,* HarperCollins, 1992, page 632.

2. Carnegie Library of Pittsburgh, Science and Technology Department, *The Handy Science Answer Book,* Visible Ink Press, page 59.

Chapter 40: How's the Air in There?

1. *Questions About Your Community: Indoor Air,* [online], [cited August, 2004], Environmental Protection Agency, Region 1 New England, www.epa.gov/region1/communities/ indoorair.html

2. E. Willard Miller and Ruby Miller, *Indoor Pollution,* ABC-CLIO Press, 1998, page 2.

3. The National Environmental Trust, *Cabinet Confidential,* July, 2004.

4. G.B. Leslie and F.W. Lunau, *Indoor Air Pollution, Problems and Priorities,* Cambridge University Press, 1992, page 118.

Chapter 42: Indoor Air Repair

1. Debra Lynn Dadd, *Home Safe Home,* Jeremy Tarcher/Putnam, 1997, page 33.

Chapter 44: Air vs. Machine

1. Debra Lynn Dadd, *Home Safe Home,* Jeremy Tarcher/Putnam, 1997, page 36-37.

2. Ibid., page 37.

3. Ellen Greenfield, *House Dangerous: Indoor Pollution in Your Home and Office,* Interlink Books, 1991, page 316.

4. Dadd, *Home Safe Home,* page 37.

5. Lynn Bower, *The Healthy Household,* The Healthy House Institute, 1995, page 316.

6. Dadd, *Home Safe Home,* page 40.

7. Ibid.

8. Bower, *The Healthy Household,* page 318.

9. Ibid.

10. Dadd, *Home Safe Home,* page 38.

11. Bower, *The Healthy Household,* page 316.

12. Dadd, *Home Safe Home,* page 40.

13. Bower, *The Healthy Household,* page 318.

14. Ibid., page 319.

15. Dadd, *Home Safe Home,* page 40.

16. Bower, *The Healthy Household,* page 319.

17. Ibid.

18. Greenfield, *House Dangerous: Indoor Pollution in Your Home and Office,* page 112.

19. Dadd, *Home Safe Home,* page 38.

20. Ibid., page 40.

21. Greenfield, *House Dangerous: Indoor Pollution in Your Home and Office,* page 112.

22. Dadd, *Home Safe Home,* page 39.

23. Greenfield, *House Dangerous: Indoor Pollution in Your Home and Office,* page 113.

24. Bower, *The Healthy Household,* pages 324-325.

Chapter 45: Air Fresheners Stink

1. Euromonitor International, *Household Care in USA,* [online], [cited May 2005], September 2004,
www.euromonitor.com/Household_Care_in_USA

Chapter 46: Use the Power of Plants to Grow a Healthy Harvest of Cleaner Air

1. Dr. B.C. Wolverton, *How to Grow Fresh Air,* Penguin Books, 1996, page 21.

2. Dr. B.C. Wolverton, *How to Grow Fresh Air,* Penguin Books, 1996.

Index